Sara Wallace hands anxious m[...] that is seasoned with practica[...] peace. Peace to a worn-out mother's heart—the kind of peace that can come only from Jesus himself. In fact, she shows us over and over again how our reliance on Christ doesn't mean that we try harder or work better but that we rest in his power to equip us for the job of motherhood. All mothers should read Sara's excellent book. Each of us needs this kind reminder to trust the Lord in this high calling that we are utterly ill-equipped to handle without his presence and help.

—**Melissa Edgington**, Blogger, *Your Mom Has a Blog*

As moms, we all care for our children. We were created to care. But sometimes that care can turn into anxiety. In *Created to Care*, Sara shows anxious moms the great care God has for them and their children. Through personal stories, insightful reflections, and the truth of God's Word, she points readers to the truth of who God is and what he has done, helping anxious moms to find peace in their sovereign God.

—**Christina Fox**, Speaker; Author, *Sufficient Hope: Gospel Meditations and Prayers for Moms*; Content Editor, *enCourage*

I have always been so grateful to read Sara's thoughts on motherhood. The gospel is the foundation for what it means to be a mother. It is always through this lens that Sara's wisdom comes shining into our everyday lives, where joining all the dots can be tricky. I'm excited about this latest release!

—**Kristyn Getty**, Soloist; Composer; Hymnwriter; Coauthor, *Sing! How Worship Transforms Your Life, Family, and Church*

Created to Care invites moms to the "shalom" that their hearts desperately crave. Its Scripture-filled pages unfold the path that leads moms toward peace with God, peace within, and peace with others—especially their husbands and children. This book is exceedingly practical and gospel-centered in its application.

—**Karen Hodge**, Coordinator of Women's Ministries, Presbyterian Church in America; Coauthor, *Transformed: Life-taker to Life-giver* and *Life-giving Leadership*

Sara Wallace identifies the source of a young mom's many anxieties, then gently points to the Creator who cares for *her*. Filled with humor, counsel, and gospel insight, *Created to Care* provides nuggets of sanity to strengthen the weary and calm the worried. Highly recommended!

—**Rondi Lauterbach**, Author, *Hungry: Learning to Feed Your Soul with Christ*

When there's so much for us to fear—including our own shortcomings—*Created to Care* reaches out toward us fellow mom-travelers in kindness, pointing us over and over again to the all-sufficiency of the One who gently leads us.

—**Holly Mackle**, Editor, *Same Here, Sisterfriend: Mostly True Tales of Misadventures in Motherhood*

From day one of motherhood I have vacillated regularly between sinful control and crippling fear. I have long struggled to trust the Lord without feeling like I'm failing my children. In her book *Created to Care*, Sara Wallace not only shares these common mom struggles but also points us to the cure: entrusting both our mothering and our children to God's sovereign care. Rather than telling us to do more or be better, Sara teaches us how to move from sin and fear in motherhood to trust and confidence in Christ. I can't think of a mom who doesn't need this book.

—**Glenna Marshall**, Author, *The Promise Is His Presence: Why God Is Always Enough*

Created to

CARE

Created to
CARE

God's Truth for
Anxious Moms

SARA WALLACE

P&R
PUBLISHING
P.O. BOX 817 • PHILLIPSBURG • NEW JERSEY 08865-0817

Do you have any thoughts on this book? Consider writing a review online. The author appreciates your feedback!

Or write to P&R at editorial@prpbooks.com with your comments. We'd love to hear from you.

You can also check out www.prpbooks.com/book /created-to-care for an anxiety diagnostic quiz for moms.

❖ ❖ ❖

Printed in the United States of America

Library of Congress Cataloging-in-Publication Data

Names: Wallace, Sara, 1983- author.
Title: Created to care : God's truth for anxious moms / Sara Wallace.
Description: Phillipsburg, NJ : P&R Publishing, [2019]
Identifiers: LCCN 2019003413| ISBN 9781629956428 (pbk.) | ISBN 9781629956435 (epub) | ISBN 9781629956442 (mobi)
Subjects: LCSH: Motherhood--Religious aspects--Christianity. | Mothers--Religious life--Christianity. | Anxiety--Religious aspects--Christianity. | Peace of mind--Religious aspects--Christianity.
Classification: LCC BV4529.18 .W348 2019 | DDC 248.8/431--dc23
LC record available at https://lccn.loc.gov/2019003413

Contents

Introduction

Wired for Worry

All I've ever wanted to do was be a mom. When I was little, I asked for a baby doll for every single birthday and Christmas. Every time I got a new doll, I would push it around in a stroller, feed it, change its clothes, and put it to bed. I even asked Jesus to please not come back before I got the chance to be a real mom.

But those baby dolls were a bit deceiving. They didn't wake me up in the middle of the night. They didn't leave me with postpartum depression. They didn't have huge diaper blowouts in the middle of church or make my hair fall out or give me mastitis. They never got sick or hurt. When I became a real mom, I found that real babies are a million times sweeter—and a million times more challenging.

How could motherhood be so wonderful and so hard at the same time, I wondered? It felt wrong to admit how hard it was. I felt like I was complaining or taking this beautiful gift for granted. I loved being a mom. I loved it so much it hurt. It gave me more joy than I could have imagined—but it also exposed the depths of my weaknesses and opened a whole new world of anxiety. I had the precious gift I had waited for all my life—and now I felt that I had to do everything I could to protect it.

Motherhood does strange things to us. Maybe you've heard the news stories that go around from time to time about moms who suddenly gain superhuman strength in order to protect their kids—stories about lifting up a three-thousand-pound car or jumping over an eight-foot wall. Science describes this phenomenon as a combination of adrenaline and pain-suppressing chemicals from the brain. We more commonly refer to it as the "Mama Bear" instinct.

God is the creator of the "Mama Bear" instinct. He uniquely fitted moms to be able to protect children. Unfortunately, it is hard to turn our "Mama Bear" instincts off. We think of thousands of ways our kids could get hurt and then try to prepare ourselves for every possible scenario. In the wee hours of the night when everyone else is asleep, we lie awake worrying about whether our kids had too much sugar, whether they're making enough friends, or whether there are any spiders in their beds.

On top of what could happen to our kids, we are also keenly aware of our own shortcomings. We envision the kind of dream childhood we want our kids to have, and then we see all the ways we might manage to mess it up. We are not the moms we think they deserve.

Do you see? Anxiety and motherhood are linked for a reason. God created us to care. But he created us to care within the context of *his* perfect wisdom and *his* perfect strength—not our own. He chose weak and broken vessels to accomplish this task so that he will get all the glory.

Author C. S. Lewis offers us a unique perspective on anxiety. He writes, "Some people feel guilty about their anxieties and regard them as a defect of faith. I don't agree at all. They are afflictions, not sins. Like all afflictions, they are, if we can so take them, our share in the Passion of Christ."[1]

Do you see the challenges of motherhood as a chance to

draw closer to God and to actually share in the sufferings of Christ? Anxiety is a sin when we give it a permanent residence in our hearts and allow it to rule our thoughts. But when we refuse to accept anxiety and instead engage in warfare against it, we bring great glory to God.

Are you ready to do battle with anxiety? You can find great strength and comfort for this battle—but only in the cross. My hope and my prayer is that this book will show you the way to that comfort—that even in this unpredictable season, you can know that God is for you. And I pray that in your darkest moments of uncertainty, you will catch a glimpse of glory that will take your breath away.

Part 1

Committing Your Motherhood to God

1

Peace for Mom Guilt

Last week I came into the living room and found my four-year-old lying perfectly still, flat on his face. I was startled.

"Honey, what are you doing?" I asked.

The muffled voice from the carpet said, "Playing with my toys."

I stared at him, confused. I didn't see any toys, and he certainly didn't look like he was playing. "What toys?"

My son shifted his body slightly so I could see under his stomach. I saw two plastic snakes, three playing cards, and a Lego man peeking out. His current favorite toys.

"Why are you lying on them?" I asked.

He turned his head to face me. "I don't want anything to happen to them."

I tried to process the situation. "You're protecting your toys so you can play with them . . . but you're not playing with them. Are you having fun?"

"Yes," came the automatic response. Obviously, he was not.

I didn't understand. My son loved these toys, but he couldn't enjoy them. He couldn't bear the idea that something might happen to them (or that a brother might dare to touch them).

He would rather lie facedown on the carpet than play with them.

I had to laugh at the ridiculousness of it. He looked so miserable. Something that was supposed to bring him joy was paralyzing him.

I have an embarrassing confession to make: that's exactly the way I sometimes feel about motherhood. I love being a mom so much, and yet it terrifies me at the same time. I suffocate my own joy by holding on too tightly. It's as ironic as my four-year-old lying on top of his favorite toys.

Does anxiety keep you from enjoying this beautiful gift of motherhood? Perhaps you have prayed, waited, and prepared to be a mom, and now you're paralyzed by the thought that something bad could happen. Or maybe motherhood caught you by surprise, and you don't feel equipped for this unexpected blessing.

We know our sin and our weakness better than anyone else. And yet God chose to entrust us with the precious gift of children. As we bask in the glorious mercy of this thought, a nagging fear creeps in: *Can I handle this? What if I mess it up?*

Before you became a mom, perhaps the consequences of your actions didn't seem so big. They usually only affected you. But now everything you do affects your kids. *Everything*— whether it's good or bad. How do you know if you're doing the right thing at any given moment? How can you protect your kids from your own weakness, incompetence, and flat-out sin?

Accepting Our Imperfection

Recently I got a sweet message from another mom. She loves her children dearly and is constantly haunted by the idea that she will mess things up for them. "I know that God can forgive me," she wrote. "But I also know that sin has consequences.

I'm afraid of what consequences my children will have to live with because I'm a sinful person."

I can relate. I know how it feels to see the hurt in my son's eyes when I speak harshly. I know what it's like to ruin everyone's fun on a family outing because I let my own stress take over. There are nights when I fall into bed with an aching heart, wishing my kids had a perfect mommy.

But they don't. And, as much as we strive to put our sin to death, there is nothing we can do to change the facts: we are sinners, and we will remain sinners until the day we are with Jesus. We will fail our children. They will live with the consequences of our sin. And you know what? *They* will be sinful parents, too. Their kids will suffer the consequences of *their* actions.

Does that sound depressing? Maybe. But, in a way, it is also freeing. Whenever I went shopping with my mom as a kid, we would listen to Elisabeth Elliot cassette tapes in the car. One of Elisabeth's favorite quotes was "In acceptance lies peace." Peace doesn't necessarily come when our circumstances change; it comes when we accept our circumstances the way they are. Does that mean we accept our sin? Yes—we accept the *fact* that we are sinners and remember that Jesus came only to save sinners (see Mark 2:17). There is peace when we stop fighting against the fact that we are sinners and say instead, "I am the one Jesus died for. Yes, I am a sinner; but I am forgiven."

Once we accept our problem, we are free to accept the solution. We know that our kids will grow up in a sinful world with sinful parents and that they will need the same solution that we do.

Accepting Christ's Perfection

When I was fourteen, a woman from my church gave a message to all the girls in the youth group. I sat in the front row and watched as she held up first a dirty old bathrobe and then her handmade wedding dress. Each handsewn bead sparkled. The girls were spellbound as she explained how Jesus removes our filthy rags and makes us his spotless bride. It was like taking off the old bathrobe and putting on a costly wedding gown. That was the first time I had ever heard the term "imputed righteousness." I knew that Jesus took my sin, but I didn't fully grasp what I got in its place: his perfect righteousness.

What does this mean for Christian mommies? It means that when God looks at us he sees his Son. Even on the bad days? On *all* the days. So often, I feel like a mess—physically, emotionally, spiritually, and mentally. I feel like the sentence "It's been one of those days" is stamped on my forehead. But God sees something else. He sees a heart that is washed white as snow—a beautiful bride waiting for him to return.

Several years after that youth group talk, I came across the verse that gives the same illustration: "I will greatly rejoice in the LORD . . . for he has clothed me with the garments of salvation; he has covered me with the robe of righteousness, as a bridegroom decks himself like a priest with a beautiful headdress, and as a bride adorns herself with her jewels" (Isa. 61:10).

These "garments of salvation" aren't something we have to put on every day. We are already wearing them. We didn't clothe ourselves; we *have been* clothed by God.

God's Part, Our Part

How do these righteous robes affect our daily motherhood? God sees his Son in me—but how does that silence the mom guilt? When we see ourselves clothed in Christ's righteousness, we have fresh confidence to do what God has called us to do. We know that he is working through us for his glory and that he will forgive us when we fail.

Connecting our theology to our daily lives doesn't always come naturally. As busy moms, we often experience a disconnect between the spiritual and the physical. Our salvation is "out there"—but the screaming baby is right in front of us. It's hard for us to meditate on eternity with Jesus when we can't see past the diapers and dishes.

We know God takes care of the "big stuff," but it's our own failure that scares us the most. We think, *Whatever God is in control of I can trust him with. But if it's in* my *control, I know I'll mess it up.* I want to encourage you: there is no separation between God's part and our part. It's *all* God's part. He is in control of every part of our motherhood—including *us.*

Yesterday I was running errands with the kids, and I turned on a sermon by one of my all-time favorite preachers: my dad. I just about slammed on the brakes when he said, "Our sins do not hinder [God's] good, eternal, sovereign purposes for you; they are part of it."[1] Amen! What kind of God can use even our sin to bring about good? What kind of grace is that? It's a grace that we don't understand. But we revel in it—and we say, "Thank you, God." I am responsible for my actions—good and bad. And God has a perfect plan for my actions—good and bad. We don't have to understand it in order to accept it—and to take great comfort from it.

I was getting my two-year-old dressed last week and marveling at his big blue eyes and his tuft of blond fluff. I thanked God for giving him to me. But I rarely (or maybe never) thank God for giving *me* to my son. Just as God picked my son for me, he picked me for my son. God chose to use me in this calling for his glory. He is working through me. When my personal insecurity nags at my heart, I can remind myself, *I have been chosen*

by God for this task. He will not leave me alone. I am forgiven. I am
new. God made me a mom for his own glory.

I first heard the word *deism* in a philosophy class in college. Deism teaches that God set the world in motion and then stepped back to let it run its course without him. Not only is this a depressing thought, it is also unbiblical. Our Creator is intimately acquainted with all our ways (see Ps. 139:3). He is the one who started the good work in us, and he has promised to complete it (see Phil. 1:6). He is walking with us every step of the way.

So often we live our lives as if God has said, "I saved you—now, you live out your life here the best you can and I'll see you on the other side." Paul calls this foolishness: "Are you so foolish? Having begun by the Spirit, are you now being perfected by the flesh?" (Gal. 3:3). God did not leave us on our own to finish what he started.

If we apply this idea to our own motherhood, it's like telling our kids, "I gave birth to you—now, you go do your thing and I'll do mine. Maybe I'll see you around some day." Don't we long to hold our kids' hands and see them through every twist and turn of their journey through childhood? That is how God deals with us, as well.

We need to mend this harmful disconnect—the idea that God handles the big stuff and we handle the rest. There is no better remedy for this than Romans 8:32: "He who did not spare his own Son but gave him up for us all, how will he not also with him graciously give us all things?" God gives us everything we need for this life. The proof? He already gave us his son.

Do you believe that God is working through you? Or do you feel like he is too far away or you are too broken? You are not just filling marching orders each day, hoping that you'll mess up a little less than the day before. You are an ambassador for Christ (see 2 Cor. 5:20). God is showing your children the gospel *through* you—and your brokenness is part of it. Let's explore how.

Not-So-Perfect Moms Share the Gospel

My kids are constantly "camping" in the house. They gather up all the lanterns and flashlights and run to the darkest place they can find (usually my closet). They head for the dark because they want their lanterns to shine brighter. In the same way, God uses our weaknesses to make his glory shine brighter. In 2 Corinthians 4:7 Paul says, "But we have this treasure in earthen vessels, so that the surpassing greatness of the power will be of God and not from ourselves" (NASB). God gets all the glory.

I can talk to my kids about God's forgiveness all day long. But showing them his forgiveness is different. When I repent in front of my kids, I take their hands and lead them to the cross. I show them the well-worn path I have walked many times. I point out my footprints for them to put their own feet in. I say, "This is where we go. This is the only path to forgiveness." I show them that glorious place where, in *Pilgrim's Progress*, Christian's burden rolled off his back and he exclaimed, "Ah, what a place is this! . . . Blessed cross! Blessed tomb! Nay, blessed is the Lord that was put to shame for me!"[2] One day, when my children recognize their sin, they will know where to go. They will remember.

Can you see how our sin is part of God's plan? God is glorified through the journey, not just at the destination. Our sin, suffering, and pain are all part of the journey. All of it points to the gospel—including our broken motherhood.

When we mess up, in both big and small ways, we can come alongside our kids and say, "We are all in this together. We are all sinners in need of a Savior." We seek our kids' forgiveness and God's forgiveness. We aren't perfect, and they won't be perfect either. We have to show them how to deal with their imperfections.

Maybe you think that your sin is too big for God to handle—that he can accomplish something good only with perfect people. Paul tells us the exact opposite: "And He has said to me, 'My grace is sufficient for you, for power is perfected in weakness.' Most gladly, therefore, I will rather boast about my weaknesses, so that the power of Christ may dwell in me" (2 Cor. 12:9 NASB).

Wait. Are we supposed to actually be *happy* about our weaknesses? Look at Paul's mixed reaction when he was smacked in the face by his sin: "Wretched man that I am! Who will deliver me from this body of death? Thanks be to God through Jesus Christ our Lord!" (Rom. 7:24–25) This same thankfulness that Paul displayed renews our own confidence for the task ahead. We have been delivered. And now we have a job to do.

Unrealistic Expectations

Speaking of jobs, have you seen the meme floating around on social media that describes a mom's job? It usually says something like "Don't tell me I don't have a job. I'm a doctor, nutritionist, chauffeur, chef, teacher, maid, accountant, counselor, project manager, and personal trainer."

The only problem is that we are *not* all of those things. We are simply women who love our babies. *None* of us could fill that kind of a job description.

When I was in school I was terrible at science. It never clicked for me. I scraped by with a passing grade, but I have accepted the fact that I will never speak periodic table. When I became a mom, suddenly I felt like I was expected to be a scientist. I was supposed to know the thousands of ingredients that were in each thing my child could possibly eat, how the ingredients would interact with each other, which nutritional elements my child should have at what age and in what quantities, when to choose homeopathic remedies and when to use modern medicine. I was a wreck.

But my expectations were crazy. Unrealistic expectations create a vicious cycle of anxiety. The only way to break the cycle is to apply God's truth directly to our expectations. What do we expect from ourselves as moms, and what does God expect from us? Let's compare job descriptions.

Our Expectations	God's Expectations
Feed my child perfect food. Never let my child get hurt. Give my child a perfect home environment. Never sin in front of my child. Give my child perfect friends. Answer all my child's questions accurately and patiently. Make every vacation scrapbook-worthy. Make every party Pinterest-worthy.	Train up a child in the way he should go (Prov. 22:6). Seek first the kingdom of God and his righteousness (Matt. 6:33). Work heartily, as for the Lord (Col. 3:23). Be faithful in the little things (see Matt. 25:21).

What differences do you notice? We get tripped up by the details, but God shows us the big picture—the end goal. To "train up a child in the way he should go" means to show our kids the gospel. Point the way to Christ over and over. We complicate things by placing expectations on ourselves that distract us from the purpose of motherhood. When we take a step back and refocus on the big picture, the details that cause us anxiety fade into the background. Suddenly we see our kids' hearts. We're reminded of what's important.

You can see how God's expectations allow for many different personality types among moms. You don't have to be good at everything. You don't have to know everything. You can point your kids to Christ whether you're a working mom or a stay-at-home mom, whether you're a college grad or a high-school dropout, whether you were raised in a Christian home or became a Christian later in life. When you start to feel the panic of not knowing how to do everything "right" for your kids, remind yourself of your simple goal: Seek first God's kingdom. Look for ways to show your kids the gospel.

This should bring so much relief to us moms. Show my kids the gospel? Yes, I can do that. Imperfectly, of course—but as we've already seen, our imperfections are part of the gospel story. We are imperfect mommies raising imperfect kids in an imperfect world. There are so many things we *don't* know, but we can cling to what we *do* know: Jesus died for sinners. Can I give my child a perfect diet? No. Can I teach him about Jesus? Yes. Big sigh of relief.

Take one more look at the expectations chart. We could fail every single one of our own expectations on the left and still fulfill God's expectations. Yep—even when we sin. And some family vacations stink. Some birthday parties are a hot mess. It doesn't mean we are failing as moms. Everything we experience with our kids, good and bad, can be part of "training them up" in the gospel.

Past, Present, and Future Comfort

A good friend in college confided in me that she was nervous about having kids one day. "I don't know what a good mom looks like," she said. She didn't come from a Christian home, and she herself didn't become a Christian until she was an adult. She already felt guilty for letting her kids down, and she didn't even have kids yet.

The hope for a mom from a non-Christian home is the same as for a mom from a Christian home: We are forgiven in Christ. We are a "new creation. The old has passed away; behold, the new has come" (2 Cor. 5:17). We have all been saved from the same dead state by the same perfect righteousness.

The disciple Peter had a messed-up track record. He denied Christ, gave in to peer pressure, and set his heart on earthly things. But he belonged to Christ. Before Peter's greatest betrayal, Christ gave him a special charge that must have echoed in his heart for the rest of his life: "I have prayed for you that your faith may not fail. And when you have turned again, strengthen your brothers" (Luke 22:32).

Christ knows that we, like Peter, will fail. But he also knows that our faith will go on. It will experience the painful flames of refining, but, in the end, it will come forth as gold. And as failed, redeemed mamas, we are called to turn and strengthen one another. Know that every mom, no matter her past, is afraid of failing her kids. When your past threatens to steal your joy, find another mom to encourage. Tell her, "We are in this together. We were dead, and now we're alive—and our kids are going to know it." This is where we see the beauty of the body of Christ. Dive into your local church. Seek out moms whom you trust and admire. You are not alone.

Do you believe that God made you a mom on purpose? Do

you believe that he put your kids in your home for a reason? If you do, then you must believe that he already knew what he was working with: a flawed mommy. Not only did he know, but he has worked your sin into the equation from the beginning. God has no Plan B. He didn't say, "Well, I need a perfect mom for this job, but you'll have to do." He chose you for your kids and your kids for you—all for his glory.

Satan does not want us to be confident. He wants us to constantly wallow in our weaknesses and insecurities so we won't show our kids the glory of Christ. I love Martin Luther's response to this: "When the devil throws our sins up to us and declares that we deserve death and hell, we ought to speak thus: 'I admit that I deserve death and hell. What of it? . . . For I know One who suffered and made satisfaction in my behalf. His name is Jesus Christ, the Son of God. Where he is, there I shall be also.'"[3]

We can accept all our inadequacies with confidence, because we've been forgiven. Our strength comes from Christ, not from ourselves. Give your insecurities to Christ. Fix your eyes on Christ in whatever he calls you to do today, and let your kids' eyes follow your gaze.

What Other Moms Are Saying

In our weakest moments of motherhood, we long to hear a voice say, "Me too!" There is comfort in knowing that we are not alone—that other moms understand the unique struggles of this season. I've been blessed to be surrounded by wise, godly mamas at every stage of my motherhood journey. At the end of each chapter, in this "What Other Moms Are Saying" section, we will have the privilege of hearing from many of these women. Some of these women I have known since grade school, when we would daydream about what it would be like to be moms and what we wanted to name our kids. Others I've met in church, at college, or through my blog. Each one has poured into my motherhood in a special way. I love the variety of perspectives they offer. I hope you will, too. Let's listen in to how other moms from all walks of life find peace in the chaos.

I am most overwhelmed when my focus is on myself. I am most equipped to be the mom I want to be when my focus in on Christ. (Rebecca)

When my husband started med school and I was on my own with the kids, another mom encouraged me to start praying more. At first I rolled my eyes—but I felt convicted about it, so I took her advice. WOW! I instantly saw a difference in my personal insecurities. I can now tell when my prayer life is lacking by how strong my personal insecurities are. (Carrie)

I think what would've helped me in my first years was for someone to just remind me that Christ is the perfect parent on my behalf and that no matter how I mess up, he alone can save my kids. (Katie)

When insecurity starts to take over, I blast worship music. My kids love it, and it helps me refocus. It's hard to grumble while singing praise. (Melissa)

I try to remember that God saw fit to make me my kids' mother and that now my kids are my mission field because God has *sent* me to them. (Jori)

When I lean on my own skills and knowledge, I stumble. That's when I remember to acknowledge *him* in all my ways (see Prov. 3:6). (Christy)

It really helps me to just have honest conversations with the Lord in which I admit all the ways I'm struggling. Something like, "Lord, I am really struggling with not getting frustrated when my daughter whines. Please give me wisdom in my parenting and honor my sincere efforts to raise her in your love and truth." (Rebecca)

When I had my twins, I was completely overwhelmed by personal insecurity. That's when I fell in love with Psalm 56:9: 'This I know, that God is for me." If a believer truly believes that, they can face anything. (Andrea)

Reflection

1. What are some unrealistic expectations you place on yourself that lead to insecurity?
2. What do you think Paul meant when he said, in 2 Corinthians 12:10, "When I am weak, then I am strong"? For more context, read verses 9–11 as well.
3. Look at the first part of Isaiah 50:9: "Behold, the Lord GOD helps me; who will declare me guilty?" How could this verse bring you comfort when you feel the "mom guilt" creeping in?
4. Look again at Luke 22:32: "I have prayed for you that your faith may not fail. And when you have turned again, strengthen your brothers." Can you think of a time in your life when you were able to use your failure as an opportunity to point someone else to Christ?
5. Do you know a mom who struggles with insecurity in motherhood? How could you encourage her today?

2

Peace in Exhaustion

My husband loves Bob Newhart. In one of his comedy sketches, Bob plays a therapist who counsels a young woman. She has all kinds of paralyzing fears, such as getting buried alive, relationships, and germs. After she opens up about each one of her fears, Bob gives her his famous advice: "Stop it!" Of course, the woman isn't happy about this. If it were that easy, she would have "stopped it" a long time ago. But Bob insists that's all she needs to do in order to cure her worry.

As ridiculous as his advice sounds, solving our problems really is that simple. Just stop it. But we know, just like the frustrated woman in the sketch, that *simple* doesn't mean *easy*. We might know in theory that we should just stop worrying, but in reality that seems impossible to do.

It seems especially impossible when we are exhausted. Sleep deprivation is one of the most painful realities of motherhood. It takes energy to fight anxiety, and energy is the one thing we often lack. We're desperate for fuel—something that will help us feel, if not our best, at least human again. Where do we get this fuel?

Our physical limitations remind us that we need supernatural help. Before we reach for the coffee pot, we need to reach for God's character.

God's Character and My Anxiety

Therapist Bob had a special cure-all phrase for anxiety: "Stop it." In the Bible, God has a special phrase, too. When Moses questions God about delivering his people from Pharaoh, God answers his fears with two words: "I Am." Unlike therapist Bob's cure, God's cure carries much more weight. It's rooted in his own character. When God says he will take care of us, he stakes his own reputation on it. We can rest in him—not because of how strong our faith is but because of how strong *he* is.

"I Am" is all we need to know in order to never fear again. But, like Moses, we are forgetful and shortsighted. We need daily (and sometimes momently) reminders of who God is. Look at how each part of God's character can silence our anxiety:

- *God is omnipotent (all-powerful)*: He is more powerful than any pain or trial that can come into my life.
- *God is loving*: His steadfast love for me will never change.
- *God is omnipresent (everywhere)*: I am never alone.
- *God is omniscient (all knowing)*: God knows the past, present, and future, and he has orchestrated all things for my good.
- *God is immutable (unchanging)*: When everything around me is uncertain, God's love and power are the same forever.
- *God is merciful*: In Christ, I am completely forgiven. God will never hold my sin against me.
- *God is holy*: He is completely perfect and worthy of my trust in every way.

- *God is just*: He will never do anything against his holy will.
- *God is all glorious*: He created me for his glory, and I can find complete satisfaction in living to please him.

God's character is our fuel. His character breathes life into verses like Philippians 4:6: "Do not be anxious about anything, but in everything by prayer and supplication with thanksgiving let your requests be made known to God."

This verse doesn't mean much if you don't know God. You'll be searching your brain for that switch to turn off your anxiety, and you won't find it. But if you do know him, you have access to the deepest comfort in the universe. The great "I Am" not only knows what you're going through; he is *for* you. The God of the universe is on your side.

This puts our worries in a whole new light. We can say with Paul, "If God is for us, who can be against us? He who did not spare his own Son but gave him up for us all, how will he not also with him graciously give us all things?" (Rom. 8:31–32).

You might be looking at your life and thinking, *It doesn't look like God is for me. And it certainly doesn't look like he has given me "all things."* If you are looking at your circumstances for proof of God's love, you are looking in the wrong place. The proof of God's love for us is not in our circumstances. It's in a person. That proof is Jesus. We know that God loves us because he gave us his only Son. If King David had looked at his circumstances, he would have had every reason to despair. But in the midst of constant spiritual attacks and physical threats, he was able to say, "This I know, that God is for me. . . . What can man do to me?" (Ps. 56:9, 11).

If you do not know for certain that God is for you, you *can* know today. Trust in Jesus Christ alone for salvation. If Christ is your Savior, you are safe in him. You can know that he lived a perfect life in your place and that he took the punishment you deserved. Now no one can snatch you out of his hand (see John 10:28).

This doesn't mean that all your worries will evaporate and never come back. But there is a difference between what we *feel* and what we *know*. Even on days when we feel anxious or discouraged, we can know that God is for us and that he has a plan for us. And we can use what we know to dramatically impact how we feel.

Right now you might be feeling like you're running on empty. You might be wondering if you have enough energy to make it through the day and if you'll ever feel rested again. Cling to what you know about God. Pick one of his character traits from the list we just looked at and say it over and over today. Your strength might waver today, and your body might fail. But you can say with Asaph, "My flesh and my heart may fail, but God is the strength of my heart and my portion forever" (Ps. 73:26).

Facing Our Physical Limitations

I remember the woman who made me terrified of becoming a mother. My husband and I were newlyweds, and we had just started attending a small-group study through our church. One of the other families who attended had four small children, who were all close in age. Every time they came to the study, the mom and dad couldn't keep their eyes open. The mom just stared blankly at the study leader and groaned every time she had to get up to chase the children. One time, I answered a question in the group and she looked at me wistfully and said, "I remember when I used to have thoughts like that. Now I can't think at all." When I looked at her, I saw my future.

I was scared. I couldn't relate to the level of exhaustion she was experiencing. But I would learn soon enough. I would walk that sleep-deprived road five times with five babies. I myself would become that bedraggled, blankly staring lady who scared all the young women in the church into never wanting kids.

Now I can look back on that season and laugh at the craziness. I've come out the other side—with a few more wrinkles and gray hairs, but wiser and more thankful. I'm sleeping again. I have energy. If you are in a season of sleep deprivation, you will laugh one day. You will tell your kids, "I was so tired, when I had you, I put my phone in the fridge. I forgot the words to 'Jesus Loves Me.' I put olive oil in my coffee instead of vanilla. I tried to put a bib on Daddy. I told the dog to say, 'Yes, Mom.' I tried reheating my coffee in the fridge. I threw poopy diapers in the hamper instead of the trash. I shaved one leg twice and the other not at all. I ran all over the house trying to find you and then found you nursing on my breast. I tried to give Grandpa a pacifier. I started the dryer with nothing in it. I dialed phone numbers and forgot who I was calling. I made choo-choo sounds whenever I saw a train, even if I was completely alone. Trust me—we're all very lucky to be here today."

I thought I knew what sleep deprivation was when I was in college. I had no idea. When my first baby was four weeks old, I got into a horrible cycle of insomnia. My postpartum hormones were out of control, and the roots of anxiety strangled out every opportunity for me to sleep. I would put the baby down for the night and lie in my bed staring at the clock. I knew I would have a couple of hours at best before the baby woke up to eat. As the minutes ticked by, I pictured my stores of strength and vitality for the next day draining away. I knew I would have nothing left. But what could I do? It was like watching someone siphon gas out of my tank, and there was nothing I could do about it. *Nothing.* I felt completely helpless. Sometimes I had panic attacks, and I had to get up and pace just to try to slow my heart rate.

I begged God to let me sleep. "Don't you know I need this?" I pleaded. "How can I do what you called me to do if I can't sleep?" I was confused. Being a mom was hard enough. How could I do it with no sleep?

It is true that we need sleep. Sleep doesn't just mean energy; it means sanity, clarity, emotional and mental stability, a healthy appetite, quick reflexes, and a host of other things that we take for granted when we are well rested. Sleep is a good gift from God. We have a loving Creator who graciously "gives to his beloved sleep" (Ps. 127:2). God does not treat our physical needs lightly. He is the one who created us with these needs, and he delights in meeting them. When we cry out to him for help, he does not despise our prayers (see Ps. 102:17). It is not wrong to be in need. It brings God glory when we recognize him as the source of all our help.

But, as it happens with many good gifts that meet our needs, this one had become an idol to me. In my heart I told God, "I cannot trust your care for me unless I have sleep." My hope was in the gift, not in the Giver. The harder I tried to hold on to sleep, the less sleep I got. I was like my toddler who once held white-knuckled onto a sharp stick as I removed it from his hands to keep him safe. God was showing me my idol. He was prying my hands open to make me let go of my dangerous self-reliance.

Our Limitless God

It's easy for us to say we trust that God can do all things when things are going well. We don't realize that we have placed limitations on him until those limitations are tested. "God can help me through the day (as long as I get a good night's sleep)." I didn't even realize that that was in my heart. I was adding conditions to my trust in God. By taking away sleep he was graciously taking away those conditions. He was showing me that he *is* enough. I love the way Kristin Tabb writes about this in her article on Desiring God:

> Exhaustion becomes a steering wheel that drives us toward God in a different way than sleep does. Sleeplessness causes us to look away from ourselves—our capacity, our resources, our energy reserve, our mental acumen, our physical strength, and our careful planning and scheming—and it causes us to rely solely on him who "does not faint or grow weary" (Isaiah 40:28). It is there, in the middle of the night, with the baby—or computer, or hospital IV, or mental stressor—that we find ourselves coming to the end of ourselves. And the end of ourselves is a very good place to be. [1]

I realized that I was terrified of what I would find if I truly came to the end of myself. I didn't want to know. But God didn't give me a choice. Sleeplessness brought me to the end of my road, and I had to stare my utter helplessness in the face. But instead of finding a black hole of despair, I found the grace of God. In those lonely hours of the night, I found a tender Father who "inclined his ear to me" (Ps. 116:2). I had never felt weaker in my life than in those first few sleepless months. And that's where God forced me to see that there is nothing wrong with being weak. It is when we are weak that God's power is perfected in us (see 2 Cor. 12:9). When we are weak, then we are strong—even when God strips away more than we've bargained for.

There was someone else who was called to a monumental

task as God stripped away every resource. Gideon faced the task of defeating the Amalekites and Midianites, whose soldiers were as numerous as locusts and whose camels were like the sand on the seashore (see Judges 7:12). Gideon had a great army, too. He had thirty-two thousand men. Sure, he was a little outnumbered, but he could handle it.

But God didn't want Gideon outnumbered. He wanted him completely defenseless. "The people with you are too many for me to give the Midianites into their hand, lest Israel boast over me, saying, 'My own hand has saved me'" (Judges 7:2). God wanted all the glory for this victory. He stripped down Gideon's army—first to ten thousand and then to a ridiculous, measly three hundred. From a human standpoint, this was a no-brainer. Gideon was toast.

But God doesn't depend on numbers. He holds *all* the cards *all* the time. Gideon won that battle—and God got all the glory (see Judges 7:19–23).

Do we trust God to equip us for the tasks that he calls us to? The duties of motherhood can seem as numerous as the locusts and as vast as the sand on the sea. Sleep seems like a pretty obvious necessity for winning this battle. But that's purely from a natural, human standpoint. God specializes in the *super*natural. When he called me to be a mom and gave me my marching orders, I didn't need to hand him a list of *his* marching orders, too. "You must give me sleep, physical strength, energy, clarity of mind, and emotional stability. Then I can do this." Instead I should have said, "All I need is you." When God gave Mary the task of bearing his Son, she didn't ask for a supply list. She said, "Behold, I am the servant of the Lord; let it be to me according to your word" (Luke 1:38).

We could not have this kind of confidence if we didn't trust that God is completely in control. There is comfort in knowing that God is sovereign over sleeplessness. When you're lying in your bed and your heart starts to race, remind yourself, "God doesn't just *know* that I won't get much sleep tonight. He *planned* it." Sleeplessness reminds us just how little control we actually have over our lives. But it doesn't touch God's control. He's not surprised or derailed or stressed out. The God who knows the number of the hairs on our heads (which, if you're like me, is significantly lower since having babies) and knows the number of the stars and calls them each by name (see Ps. 147:4; Matt. 10:30)—that very same God has planned exactly how much sleep we will get each night, down to the last second.

What's more comforting still is that God's plans always have a purpose. He promises his people that his plans for us are for our "welfare and not for evil" and to give us "a future and a hope" (Jer. 29:11). In Christ, we can rest in our promise-keeping God. Not only does he know about our trials, he has worked them into our lives for our good and his glory.

That doesn't mean that they won't be painful. God gave us sleep for a reason, and when we don't get it we suffer greatly. But in my own sleepless nights and the torturous days that followed, I saw God's mercy. It was raw, and it was real. There were days when I couldn't see anything *but* God's mercy. Every foot that I put in front of the other was God's mercy. I saw his mercy in friends and family who provided food when I could barely remember where the fridge was. I saw his mercy in random naps I was able to take at completely unplanned times. I saw his mercy in coffee. I saw his mercy in extra prayer time. I saw his mercy in verses that had been hidden in my heart for years and that suddenly came alive to hold me tight when I felt like I was falling through thin air.

Sleeplessness has stripped me of all my strength time and again, but it has never destroyed me. No matter how weak my body, my mind, or even my faith, God has been "the strength of my heart and my portion forever" (Ps. 73:26). My flesh and my heart have failed me many times—but God has never failed me.

This sleepless stage of life is a great reminder of things that are guaranteed—and things that are not. I am not guaranteed a good night's sleep. And I'm not just talking about during this phase of life; I mean *ever*. Yes, I might sleep better when my kids are grown. But I might not. Sleep is never a guarantee. God doesn't owe it to me. That might sound horribly discouraging, especially if you are in a sleepless stage right now, but hang on with me. I want to show you comfort that runs deeper than simply outlasting a particular stage. There is something that *is* guaranteed to us, right now, with sleep or without sleep:

> But this I call to mind,
>   and therefore I have hope:
>
> The steadfast love of the LORD never ceases;
>   his mercies never come to an end;
> they are new every morning;
>   great is your faithfulness. (Lam. 3:21–23)

I love that that verse uses the word *morning*. As a sleep-deprived mom, I find mornings especially grueling. But that's exactly where God meets me with fresh mercy. I might not feel "new" every morning, but God's mercies are always new. My energy might be small (or non-existent), but God's faithfulness is *great*. My feet might be wobbly, but God's love is *steadfast*. When I call these truths to my mind, I have hope that pushes through my exhaustion.

What Other Moms Are Saying

I used to go straight to the TV or to social media, but now when I can't sleep I start by counting my blessings. It helps me to turn my thoughts to God and positive things. (Christel)

I've learned to find peace in my spiritual rest in Jesus, even when I do not have physical rest. This reminds me that I have everything I need in him, even when I feel weak. (Kim)

I play the alphabet game, like I do with the kids. I go through the alphabet and thank God for something that starts with each letter. (Janet)

I like to practice muscle-relaxing techniques and diffuse essential oils. I also like to pick a prayer buddy to pray for at night, and then I can know she is praying for me, too. (Emily)

I use my awake-at-night time to listen to Christian podcasts. (Juliana)

In my darkest nights, I sing praise songs. I ask God to help me surrender to his will for that moment. (Bethany)

Praying for others gets my mind off myself. Otherwise I can start to feel sorry for myself because of my lack of sleep. (Brenda)

Reflection

1. What are some specific ways God has shown you mercy in sleeplessness?

2. Read Psalm 121 below and underline all the ways the Lord protects his people. (This includes what he *will* do and what he *will not* do.)

> I lift up my eyes to the hills.
>> From where does my help come?
> My help comes from the LORD,
>> who made heaven and earth.
> He will not let your foot be moved;
>> he who keeps you will not slumber.
> Behold, he who keeps Israel
>> will neither slumber nor sleep.
> The LORD is your keeper;
>> the LORD is your shade on your right hand.
> The sun shall not strike you by day,
>> nor the moon by night.
> The LORD will keep you from all evil;
>> he will keep your life.
> The LORD will keep
>> your going out and your coming in
>> from this time forth and forevermore.

3. Look back through the chapter and highlight all the Scripture passages that were mentioned. Choose one to memorize and meditate on during the night. Write it here.

4. From these passages, make a list of three guarantees you can depend on, no matter what stage of life you're in.

5. Do you know another mom of little ones? Write her name here, along with a prayer that God will give her the gift of sleep and the gift of knowing his strength and mercy. Write her a note letting her know that you prayed for her.

3

Peace in Prioritizing God, Marriage, and Kids

A couple of years ago I came across an article that started, "Dear Mom on the iPhone . . ."

Oh boy, I thought. *Here we go again.* I sighed and prepared myself for a guilt trip. I'm often that mom on her cell phone. But this time I was in for a surprise. The article wasn't guilt-tripping moms for looking at their phones. The author, Jennifer Hicks, said that she understands. She said that she knows why the mom at the park isn't watching every twirl and jump and spin: "You're not watching . . . because you just spent every waking hour before arriving at the park watching everything your child did. Every. Little. Thing."[1]

Can our phones sometimes be a distraction from what's important? Of course. But this article gave me a fresh perspective. We stare at our kids all day long. We listen to every sound; we smell every smell. Our brains are on overdrive trying to synthesize all the information in order to make sure our kids are getting what they need.

But *sometimes*, heaven forbid, we have to look away. We

have to check social media for updates on a sick friend. We have to compare prices in grocery ads and look up recipes that will use up the last few random ingredients in the fridge. (Can I make a casserole using only condiments?) We have to check the budget app, plan a birthday party, and check when the library books are due.

Jennifer Hicks says, near the end of her article, "There's a lot that demands our attention in this parenting life—and a lot that we want to soak in and enjoy. There's also a lot that happens in our lives outside of parenting that we cannot neglect. While parenting might be our most important and rewarding job, it's not the only one."

If you're a mom, you wear a lot of hats. In addition to being a mom, perhaps you are also an employee, a sister, a wife, a daughter, a church member, and a friend. You are constantly dividing up your time, your attention, your energy, and even your heart. If you're like me, your conclusion is "There's just not enough of me to go around."

If that's where we left it, things would be pretty depressing. It would mean that no matter how hard we worked, it would never be enough. But that's not where we have to leave it. Yes, we are limited—but God is not. There might not be enough of "me" to go around, but there is *more* than enough grace.

If you are constantly wondering how to prioritize, whether you're doing enough, or even *what* you should be doing, there is one answer that can lay all your worries to rest: *do the will of God.* No matter where you are or what you're doing, you can always do God's will. How? By being faithful to whatever he has placed in front of you. This takes all the guesswork out of what you "should" be doing. What's right in front of you? If you're like me, it's probably a little person in the bathroom waiting to be wiped. Maybe it's a pile of laundry or a friend who needs a phone call. Maybe it's nothing like what you thought you'd be doing in this phase of your life. But if it's right in front of you, then it's God's will for you.

Does this give you a sense of relief? This means that even if all your plans fall apart, you can still do God's will. You can still bring him glory. You can go to bed at night and assure yourself, "This day went nothing like what I had planned—but it went exactly the way it was supposed to."

I had to remind myself of that today. I planned a park day with a friend I hadn't seen in a while. I thought it would be a great chance to catch up. But moments after we arrived, things fell apart. My toddler took off for the jungle gym, and I remembered he wasn't old enough to climb without me standing several inches from him to guard the big openings. My big kids started wrestling with other kids at the park, and their parents were less than thrilled. And my middle son ran over to a tree and started barfing. Well, that was fun. Time to pack it up.

I was so disappointed. I thought that my goal was so God-honoring: to spend time with a good friend and encourage each other. Instead I spent the whole time just trying to keep my kids alive . . . and other peoples' kids safe from my kids. As I buckled my kids in the car, I wanted to cry. I thought, *What a waste. We should have stayed home. It was so hard just to get five kids here. What in the world was this all about?*

But I had to catch myself and remember, *This went exactly the way it was supposed to. I'm doing exactly what God wants me to do. I don't understand it, but I don't have to. I woke up this morning with five precious kids to take care of, and that's what I'm doing.* I felt much better as we drove home. Instead of wasting time on being disappointed, I jumped into the rest of the day.

Hudson Taylor was a missionary to China in the 1800s. He once wrote, "I am no longer anxious about anything, as I realize the Lord is able to carry out His will, and His will is mine. It makes no matter where He places me, or how. That is rather for Him to consider than for me; for in the easiest positions He must give me His grace, and in the most difficult, His grace is sufficient."[2]

Are you struggling with peace in prioritizing? Are you stuck trying to figure out what's important, what's not, and how to fit everything in? Take comfort in doing God's will. That is your number-one priority, and it has already been picked for you. The rest is just details.

So let's take a look at those details together. Let's see how doing God's will trickles down into the day-to-day workload we have as moms. It's good to take control of our priorities, but if we're not careful, our priorities can start controlling *us*. We can become slaves to our to-do lists. We can idolize the "perfect plan" and then spiral into guilt when we miss the mark.

We're going to take a look at six priorities (three in this chapter and three in the next chapter) that consume the most of our time and effort. We'll identify the big-picture goal for each category and then explore practical ways to make each goal happen.

Priority 1: God

The Big Picture

In high school and college, I started every day with Bible time. I never missed it. But when I became a mom, my time was no longer my own. The hours all ran together in an endless fog of exhaustion. My Bible reading was sporadic and disorganized. I felt out of control and anxious. It was a box that I was very nervous about leaving unchecked day after day. It wasn't just that I missed time in God's Word. I was worried that something bad would happen if I let my head hit the pillow without reading something from my Bible during the day.

My anxiety revealed something about my heart. I knew that time in God's Word was important, but I was making Bible reading an idol. Is that even possible? Yes—it's possible if our confidence is in the minutes we log in our quiet-time journals instead of in the Person with whom we are spending the time. Time in God's Word is *for* us, but it's not ultimately *about* us. It's about Christ. He is our Bread of Life (see John 6:35). He is the life-sustaining vine (see John 15:5). We come to God's Word in order to feed on our Savior.

When we make God's Word all about us, it's easy for us to be disappointed in our quiet times. If we don't get the spiritual high we are hoping for, they feel like a waste of time. If we skip them, we feel guilty. But when we remember that they're about Christ, we can rest in the work God is doing in our hearts. We adjust our expectations and enjoy our quiet times for what they really are: a long-term investment in our relationship with our heavenly Father.

During seasons of messy, sporadic quiet times, I experienced a new side of God's fatherly care. He did not leave me. On days that I cried out to him, too tired to feed myself much less read my Bible, he was faithful. That's because my relationship with him is based solely on the finished work of Christ, not on my daily spiritual disciplines. In those desperate moments, I experienced the comfort that Isaiah talks about when he says, "He will tend his flock like a shepherd; he will gather the lambs in his arms; he will carry them in his bosom, and gently lead those that are with young" (Isa. 40:11). We need to read God's Word, but we also need to trust in God's ability to keep us during this unpredictable season.

So should we even try? I want to encourage you with the assurance that every moment in God's Word is worth it. "Quiet time" might not be so quiet—but God is faithful. His Word is living and active, and it can work in us despite our fatigue and distractedness (see Heb. 4:12).

When we read God's Word, we are planting seeds in our hearts. God is the one who will bring about the growth. Paul shows us this progression in 1 Corinthians 3:6 when he says, "I planted, Apollos watered, but God gave the growth."

We can't skip the planting. We must be faithful to put God's Word into our hearts and to trust that God will be faithful to use it in our lives. There have been many times when a verse has popped into my head at just the right moment and I've thought, "When did I read that?" I don't know. But I put it in there, probably in a sleep-deprived state, and God brought it to my mind when I needed it.

The Details

How do we make our quiet times happen? Time in God's Word is important, but the details—time, place, what we read, how long we pray—will vary from season to season and from person to person. To analyze what will work best for your specific season and personality, ask yourself the following three questions.

When? When will you spend time in God's Word? Choose a specific time—whether it's a time on the clock or a chunk in the schedule—such as "whenever the baby takes an afternoon nap." Perhaps it's a few verses on your phone whenever you sit down to feed the baby. Maybe it's before the kids wake up, or right after they go to bed. Remember not to compare your Bible-reading strategy to another mom's strategy. There were years when I could not get up before my kids because I had already been up all night with an infant. I felt guilty every time I heard about another mom's 5 a.m. jog and Bible reading. Everyone's strategy is different and is based on their season and their personality.

Daily Bible reading is not one of the Ten Commandments—but there are principles that direct us to be in God's Word *often*. Colossians 3:16 tells us to let the Word of Christ dwell in us *richly*. In Psalm 1:2, David says we are blessed when we meditate on God's law day and night. God's Word should always be fresh on our minds.

A couple of years ago I heard Aimee Joseph speak about gospel-centered motherhood at The Gospel Coalition Women's Conference. Aimee has three young boys and a busy ministry and homeschool schedule. She realized that her most productive time in God's Word was a two-hour chunk of time once a week at a coffee shop. During the week she would reflect on what she had read, but she didn't have additional daily quiet times. One point that she made during the conference has always stuck with me: "If you have feasted one day, you can nibble during the week." So simple, but truly profound. One big chunk in the beginning of the week might be more productive than fifteen minutes daily during the rest of the week. The point is time with the Lord, not checking something off our to-do lists. When is the best time for you? When do you feel the least distracted and the most alert?

Where? Where will you have your quiet time? Aimee Joseph mentioned the coffee shop—her husband watched the kids once a week so she could leave the house for a couple of hours. But you don't have to leave your house in order to spend time in the Word. Choose the quietest spot in the house. It might be your bedroom, or even a closet.

What? What are you going to read? When you have a specific reading plan, you are much more likely to stick with it. If you have not had a regular quiet time before, I recommend starting with a shorter book of the Bible, like Philippians or Colossians. Then work your way up to a read-through-the Bible plan.[3] If you feel stuck in a rut in your Bible reading, pick up a Bible study book. I love the fresh perspective I get from good Bible study teachers such as Melissa Kruger and Kathleen Neilson.

God's Word and prayer are the means through which God feeds our souls. When we skip them, we don't deprive ourselves of salvation itself, but we do deprive ourselves of the *joy* of our salvation. We miss out on beautiful fellowship with God that can encourage our hearts and strengthen us against temptation and discouragement.

Priority 2: Marriage

The Big Picture

It can be challenging for us to maintain our most important relationships during motherhood. How can we strike a healthy balance? Although I'll be focusing on the marriage relationship here, many of the following strategies apply to friendships as well.

Does it feel strange to "schedule" your husband in? It doesn't have to. It simply means you've accepted the fact that quality time doesn't happen on its own. If your laundry gets its own special scheduled time with you, shouldn't your husband? One of the most loving things you can do for your husband is to purposefully invest in him.

It's a sad reality that many marriages fall apart after the kids leave the nest. Why? The parents are so focused on the kids that when the kids leave, they look at each other and can't remember why they liked each other. They don't know each other anymore.

It's easy to forget to prioritize our husbands—not because we don't love them, but because our kids are so dependent on us. If we have to choose between giving our attention to our kids or to our husbands, we might think, *He's an adult. He can take care of himself. The kids need me right now.* But that's a recipe for an unhealthy marriage. It's also not true. Just as our kids would starve if we didn't feed them, our marriages will starve if we don't invest in them.

God created marriage to be a picture of Christ and the church (see Eph. 5:22–32). Marriage, not parenting, is the ultimate picture of the gospel. God created the relationship between a husband and wife before he created children. When we prioritize our husbands, we're not just trying to keep them happy; we are putting the gospel on display for our kids.

The big picture here is our attitude toward our husbands: are we *preferring* them in love, or are we simply *pacifying* them so we can move on to the next thing? Preferring and pacifying might look the same in the moment ("Okay, I'll take five minutes to listen about your new work project"), but the difference shows. It's in our body language, our tone, our sighs, and how often we look at the clock. If we truly want to prioritize our husbands, our hearts have to be in it.

The difference between preferring and pacifying is reflected in Philippians 2:3: "Do nothing from selfish ambition or conceit, but in humility count others more significant than yourselves." Pacifying says, "What I can I do to keep him happy so I can get back to what I want to do?" Preferring says, "How can I bless my husband?"

The Details

Does this mean you should schedule weekly date nights? Maybe, but not necessarily. I remember one well-meaning couple who constantly asked us when we had gone on a date last. They thought weekly date nights were the best way to keep a marriage healthy, because that's what worked for them. At that time, I had a baby and a toddler and was three months pregnant with my next one. I panicked. "We haven't gone out on a date in two months! What's going to happen to us?"

The way you prioritize your marriage isn't about how many date nights you have. It's about quality time with your husband. This might happen with or without the kids. It might happen in person, or it might happen long-distance if your husband works away from home for weeks at a time. Look for ways to be intentional about connecting with your husband in those simple moments.

When our kids were babies, my husband would stop by the house at the end of his workday and pick us all up to run his work errands. My husband and I got to debrief about the day in the car while the babies sat quietly in their car seats. It was a refreshing reset for both of us during a very hectic season.

What speaks love to your husband? Before you make a list of special ways to invest in your marriage, consider his personality. What is his love language? What makes him feel loved and appreciated?

My husband loves having quiet time to talk to me first thing in the morning. It sets his day on the right track. I'm a "work first, talk later" kind of person, so this was not easy for me at first. But after years of starting our day this way, I can't imagine it any other way. After breakfast, we send all the kids to their rooms to play quietly while we have about an hour of "Mommy and Daddy coffee time." We discuss the day and enjoy each other's company. It has been important for me to give my husband all of my attention during this time. I don't immediately hop up when the kids start to squabble. I don't do the breakfast dishes. Interruptions still come, but I minimize them the best I can so I can prioritize this time with my husband.

We take notes on kids' allergies, fill planners with dentist appointments, and stick Post-it notes of shopping lists to the fridge. But where do we keep track of our husbands? A friend once told me she keeps a journal about her husband. She uses it to keep track of his likes and dislikes, things he would like to do, and goals that they make together.

Prioritizing your husband will bless your marriage, but it's important to remember that you aren't prioritizing your husband primarily for yourself. You're prioritizing him in order to help him be the best man God has called him to be. Sometimes this requires sacrifice. It might mean giving him time to rest when you think he should be helping around the house. It might mean helping him schedule time out with friends even if you haven't left the house in a few days.

The housework can wait a few extra minutes. The kids can watch a show. Our husbands need to know that they are important. When we prioritize our marriages, the whole family thrives.

Priority 3: Kids

The Big Picture

For most of us moms, prioritizing our kids is not difficult. We think about them all day and all night. If anything, we often prioritize them *too* much. They can quickly become the center of our universe. How can we be good stewards of these precious gifts while also balancing everything else in our lives?

When we prioritize our kids, we have one refreshingly simple big-picture goal. Ready? *Train your children up in the Lord.* We talked about this in chapter 1. A simple goal requires simple means: love, comfort, stability, predictability, and consistency. Our kids don't need constant stimulation, exotic family vacations, or a spot in every extracurricular activity. We can train up our kids in the Lord in the context of a simple, loving home.

We are talking about prioritizing our kids' hearts, not just their activities. This isn't about organizing our kids' schedules so we can squeeze in more stuff. We're seeking to prioritize the special shepherding moments that happen in regular, day-to-day life at home.

Michael Horton, author of *Ordinary*, gives parents permission to relax: "We need to take the pressure off of . . . parents, let them take a breath, and, resting in God's grace, let them revel in the ordinary chat in the car, the normal conversation over family devotions, and the countless moments that add up. Our families, including us, do not need more quality time, but more quantity time. That's when most of the best things happen . . . the things that bubble up when people are living ordinary lives together."[4]

Quantity over quality? That's the opposite of what we usually hear. But Horton's point is refreshing: our most precious moments with our kids often happen during ordinary, everyday life. This frees us up to enjoy the simple moments that are right in front of us.

What about moms who don't have the luxury of lots of "quantity" time? Some moms work outside the home. Some have joint custody. Even if you don't have lots of "quantity" time, you can still treasure the ordinary. Revel in the simple. Spend time enjoying each moment for what it is.

I love how author Harriet Connor helps us to strike this balance between quality and quantity time in her article "Give Your Children All of Your Attention. Some of the Time."[5] It's not practical to give our kids all our attention all the time—and it's not healthy for them. Connor's advice is to give our kids smaller, more concentrated doses of our attention throughout the day rather than an entire day of half-hearted, distracted attention. This lifts our burden of having to ask, "Am I spending enough time with my kids?" It's okay to tell your kids, "I'm not available right now." This teaches them so many valuable lessons: patience, thoughtfulness, selflessness, and respect. The balance here is that we should make time to *be* available. If we spend the entire day waving the kids away from us, our priorities are off balance.

The Details

The practical implications of this might come down to what we *stop* doing as parents. For starters, we can stop feeling guilty about not spending every ounce of emotional and mental energy on our kids. We can't do it. We need to accept our limitations and give our kids what we *can* give them with joy.

This will play out differently for different parents. Some parents schedule times with their kids when they can talk with them undistractedly. We've done this before at bedtime. Throughout the day I might say, "That's a great question. Let's talk about it when I tuck you in tonight."

Other times, it's as simple as making eye contact in the moment and giving a smile. When my son wants to tell me a long, complicated story about a dream he had, I have two choices. I can tell him to save it for later (and make sure that later actually happens), or I can stop what I'm doing and look him in the eye and listen. Both options show love to my son. As a third option, sometimes I dial Grandma and hand him the phone. He talks her ear off and she eats it up. It's a win-win-win situation.

Kids love to be included. They don't necessarily want to be the center of every activity; they just want to be part of regular family life. This might look like letting them help put the laundry away or help pull weeds. They can help get the home ready for company. They can quietly look at books next to you when you are reading your Bible. Enjoy their company and let them enjoy yours.

But that doesn't mean they have to be part of *every*thing, *all* the time. Kids benefit from alone time. We work "alone time" into our everyday routine. It's a time for me to take a breather from the constant needs and chatter, and it gives the kids time to think and play in peace and quiet. Part of living life together means taking breaks from one another. It's healthy for kids to have time to play alone, within an environment where they feel loved and secure.[6]

A constant prayer of mine is "Lord, help me to show love to each of my kids today in whatever way is most meaningful to them." Each of my kids absorbs love in slightly different ways. One loves physical affection. One wants to talk. One wants to show me things. Part of prioritizing our kids is *knowing* them. This helps us to shepherd their hearts in simple but deep ways. What speaks love to your child? There are so many things we could do for our kids—too many things. Choose one or two simple things each day that speak love to your child, and let the rest go. Their hearts will be full and satisfied.

Eternal Perspective

It's tempting for us to measure our success by the number of items we check off our to-do lists. But if measurable results are our fuel, we will hit burnout. So much of what we do as moms has spiritual results that we can't see. As we seek to prioritize what's important, we must "look not to the things that are seen but to the things that are unseen. For the things that are seen are transient, but the things that are unseen are eternal" (2 Cor. 4:18).

It's this eternal perspective that protects us from idolizing our to-do lists. Having this perspective is like hitting the reset button on our expectations. It makes it easier for us to see what's important. We become content with simply being faithful.

Are you willing to trust God with results you can't see? One of my favorite hymns reminds us of the beauty of letting God's glory govern our priorities:

> Turn your eyes upon Jesus,
> Look full in His wonderful face,
> And the things of earth will grow strangely dim,
> In the light of His glory and grace.[7]

What Other Moms Are Saying

Priority 1: God

One tactic I use is to read my Bible out loud to my kids during mealtime or snack time. They may not get a lot out of it, but it lets me get a bit of reading in and sets an example for them, which they don't see if I do my "regular" Bible time before they wake up. (Janet)

When our kids wake up early, we have them sit quietly and read their books while my husband and I do our devotions. (Jodie)

I listen to an audio Bible-reading plan on my phone. I listen while I get ready in the morning or on long car rides. (Holly)

Priority 2: Husband

We put our kids to bed pretty early (7 p.m.—they are ages 6, 4, and 2) even though we know they're not very tired yet and are just going to hang out in there and play. It's so good for us to start our kid-free evening time a little earlier and to have those hours together . . . even if they're full of interruptions for the first hour or two! (Laura)

Teaching the kids early that Mommy-and-Daddy time is important is as simple as saying, "Mommy is talking to Daddy right now; you can play with your toys while you wait." It takes time and consistency, but it's a good step toward showing them that they don't run the show! (Carrie)

I try to prioritize my husband in lots of small ways instead of major, planned events. No matter how you do it, it can involve more of an attitude than actual actions. When my husband gets home from work, it's easy for me to just keep working at dinner or whatever task I'm doing. If I take the time to stop what I'm doing and greet him with a hug and a kiss, he feels special and my kids recognize that he's important to me. (Rachel)

Priority 3: Kids

I include my kids in the prioritizing process. My four-year-old son and I sit down and make a list of things that he wants to do for the day. This really helps me throughout the day to take a minute to look at his list and put mine away for the moment so I can do activities with him. (Virginia)

I try to remind myself to be playful with the kids. The world will not end if I do not accomplish everything on my to-do list. (Katie)

I have started doing less juggling and more including. I include the kids in whatever I'm doing—cleaning, cooking, or reading. Instead of shooing them out of the way, I've been taking time to explain what I'm doing so that it becomes a teaching opportunity. (Julie)

Reflection

1. Read these verses from Ecclesiastes 3. How do they affect your perspective on priorities? "For everything there is a season, and a time for every matter under heaven. . . . He has made everything beautiful in its time. . . . So I saw that there is nothing better than that a man should rejoice in his work, for that is his lot" (vv. 1, 11, 22).

2. For each of the three categories we discussed in this chapter, identify its big-picture goal and one practical way you could achieve it.

Priority: **God**

Big-picture goal:

How to achieve it:

Priority: **Husband**

Big-picture goal:

How to achieve it:

Priority: **Kids**

Big-picture goal:

How to achieve it:

4

Peace in Prioritizing Home, Church, and Self

The last time I went school shopping for my kids, I passed by the aisle of planners. They always look so pretty—so crisp and fresh. There are so many to choose from: daily, weekly, monthly, spiral-bound, journal-style. . . . They beckon to me, saying, "Come and get your life together. Get more out of your day. Be more accomplished."

The older I get, the more appreciation I have for planners. I can't hold everything in my brain. I love to get it out of my brain and onto paper. But as much as I love a good planner, a good perspective has always served me even better. My friend Bethany recently gave me some advice on planning. She said, "Every morning when I wake up, I ask myself, 'Who am I living to please today?'"

No matter how well or how poorly I plan, I can have a successful day if I am living to please the Lord. He knows that I have a lot on my plate. He gave it to me! He also knows all of my limitations. On the days when I feel the most overwhelmed, I open my hands to him and say, "Take my work and glorify yourself. It all belongs to you anyway." There is so much peace in acknowledging that all things are "from him and through him and to him" (Rom. 11:36).

In this chapter, we'll take a look at three more priorities that we juggle on a daily basis: the home, the church, and ourselves.

Priority 4: Home

The Big Picture

Home is our refuge. It's our place to recuperate. It should be our family's favorite place to be. But there is no absolute standard for what the home should *look* like. Home is where we as moms create an environment of contentment, peace, and joy for our families. We can create this environment whether we live in a mansion or a studio apartment.

The book of Proverbs refreshes our perspective on homemaking. A humble home with peace is better than a wealthy home full of strife (see Prov. 17:1). The corner of the roof is a better place to live than a house with a quarrelsome wife (see Prov. 25:24). A wise woman can build a thriving home (see Prov. 14:1).

Our big-picture goal is to create beautiful homes from the inside out. Our attitudes set the tone for our homes. What does that look like?

The Details

Our homes, first and foremost, should bless our families. What makes our kids and husbands comfortable? What recharges them?

Last week, my four-year-old zipped past me with an armload of stuffed animals. I asked him where he was going, and he said, "We're camping in your closet!" I groaned. My closet had been a catch-all for several weeks' worth of laundry and school books. "Oh, honey. It's such a mess in there." He smiled and said, "It's not a mess, Mom. It's cozy." I peeked into the closet to see what he meant. Sure enough, there were stuffed animals tucked into the little hills and valleys made by the piles of clean laundry waiting to be folded. My four-year-old had burrowed into a pile himself and was busily caring for his "family" of stuffed monkeys and dinosaurs.

"It's not messy; it's cozy." That one sweet little comment revolutionized the way that I thought about my home. If the kids are cozy, then my home is serving its purpose. Of course, a four-year-old's definition of "cozy" is different from mine, so we compromise. We should all be cozy.

Second, our homes should be a blessing to others. What makes others feel welcome and comfortable in our homes? I love having people over, but I hesitate to extend that blessing when my floor is sticky and the only clean dishes have Star Wars characters on them. In one of my all-time favorite articles by Jen Wilkin, she shares the subtle but heart-changing differences between blessing and impressing: "Entertaining is always thinking about the next course. Hospitality burns the rolls because it was listening to a story. Entertaining obsesses over what went wrong. Hospitality savors what was shared. Entertaining, exhausted, says 'It was nothing, really!' Hospitality thinks it was nothing. Really. Entertaining seeks to impress. Hospitality seeks to bless."[1]

I recently went to a friend's house and noticed that her sink was full of dishes, just like mine. I was at her house because, instead of making time for her dishes, she was making time for *me.* And it blessed my socks off. It was a great reminder to me that a well-kept home is not an end unto itself. It is for the benefit of other people.

How do you know if your home is a blessing to your family

and others? Some moms might need to put the Norwex cloth down and relax. Others will need to dig themselves out of the filth and make a plan. Where do we start, and when is it clean *enough*?

Here are six questions you can consider to help you make your home a blessing.

1. *What's important to your husband?* Ask your husband what his priorities are for the home, and do those first.
2. *Could you pick it up in ten minutes?* If everything has a place and smaller deep-cleaning jobs get done throughout the week, the house can be reasonably picked up at a moment's notice.
3. *Are basic needs being met?* Make sure that everyone has clean underwear before you alphabetize the DVD collection.
4. *Could someone else step in and run your home for a day?* Look for ways to make your home efficient and self-explanatory in case of emergencies.
5. *Are important things easily accessible?* A tidy home should be an *easy* home. Don't hide the pens and toilet paper just because they don't look nice.
6. *Are you keeping up or catching up?* Tidy up a little bit all day long rather than doing it in big chunks. This keeps the home efficient and always ready for the next thing.

Priority 5: Church

The Big Picture

One Sunday, shortly after I had my first baby, my husband and I slid into our seats in the back of the church. I had my newborn bundled up in his car seat beside me. I was pretty proud of us for making it there. But I wondered why it was so quiet.

Everyone was seated, and the pastor was in mid-sentence. A lady next to me beamed at me and said quietly, "It's so good that you came." I smiled back, wondering why she was so impressed. And then I heard the pastor say, "Let's close in prayer."

We had actually arrived an hour late. We were so sleep-deprived that we forgot what time the service started. After all that effort, we just turned around and went back home. But at least the lady next to us thought we had tried our best, bless our hearts.

I can laugh about it now, but at the time, I thought, *What are we doing? Going to church is so difficult right now. Is it even worth it?*

Before we can talk about going to church, we have to understand what it means to *be* the church. If you are a Christian, you are part of the people of God. It is part of your new identity in Christ. We are saved individually, but we are also saved to a body. Look at the beautiful group language Peter uses in 1 Peter 2:9: "But you are a chosen race, a royal priesthood, a holy nation, a people for his own possession." This is a foreign concept to our individualistic culture. But we find so much strength and comfort when we accept our shared identity as the people of God, rather than simply individual *persons* of God. God chose the local church to be our means of living out this identity.

Megan Hill reminds us that our roles as mothers "do not eclipse our identity in the eternal family of God. As Christian women, we are the children of God (Gal. 4:6), mothers and sisters to the fellow-members of our local church (1 Tim. 5:2; see also Titus 2:3–5), and part of Christ's beloved bride (Rev. 21:9). If ever you say to yourself, *I'm the mom of three young kids! I'll get back to church in a few years*, you've had your identity stolen."[2]

Motherhood is not a season for us to take a break from church. It is a season for us to dive in deeper and draw strength from our identity as the bride of Christ. This refreshes our perspective when we are tempted to think, *I'm too tired to get anything out of the sermon. It will throw off my baby's nap. My kids are too distracting. There's too much to catch up on at home.* All this might be true, but we're there for a bigger purpose.

The Details

I remember one pastor saying, "When you miss church, the church misses you." At the time I laughed and thought, "They're not missing much. I'm a mess right now." But the church needs our messes. Our messes put God's grace and strength on display.

When going to church is difficult, bring the difficult with you. Pastor Scott Slayton of Chelsea Village Baptist Church in Alabama says, "Since the church is a family, when you don't gather with them there is an empty seat at the table. The church is a temple and you are a brick in it, so the whole structure is weaker and more vulnerable when you are not there."[3]

It was difficult getting my first newborn ready for church, and it is still difficult getting five little boys ready and out the door. I have to tell them to look at the pastor and stop licking the hymnals. But when I see my sisters in Christ sitting around me, bouncing babies on their knees and pointing out words in their Bibles for their kids to follow along, my heart is strengthened. I look around and think, *This is* real *life. We're all in this together.*

I'm not here to kick you when you're down and tell you to get your act together. I want to comfort you with the fact that you are part of something much bigger than your current circumstances. You're not alone. You are part of a body, a temple, a family. You need the church, and the church needs you.

Do you bring your kids to church by yourself? Don't be afraid to ask for help. You could be a huge blessing to someone else in the body by giving them an opportunity to help you. Arrange to have a friend meet you there and sit with your family or help take your kids to their classes. Ask an older woman if she could be available to hold your baby whenever you take the toddler to the bathroom. The body thrives when we work together.

So on Saturday night, set out your kids' church clothes and put some snacks in the diaper bag. Put the Bibles by the front door. Set the alarm and make the best church plan you can. And if all your plans fall apart—like mine often do—there's still a seat for you at the table. There's a place card for "tired, late moms of littles," and the body of Christ is blessed when that spot is filled.

Priority 6: Self

The Big Picture

One day, when we were driving, my husband and I saw a bumper sticker that said, "If mama ain't happy, ain't nobody happy." My husband smiled at me and said, "Yep."

It's true. As moms, we are the hub of the home. Our attitudes affect our families more than anything else that we do—more than keeping a clean home or cooking healthy meals or taking them to the park. When life feels chaotic and your home and schedule are a far cry from what you want them to be, you can give your kids joy simply through a reassuring smile and a thankful heart.

When I first heard the term *self-care*, I cringed. We're not supposed to think about ourselves, are we? Isn't that being selfish and self-centered? But self-care isn't ultimately about us. It's about using the best of ourselves for the people we love. We get to pour ourselves out for our families (see Phil. 2:17)—but if we're empty, we'll have nothing to pour. We can't care for others if we don't care for ourselves.

Self-care sounds logical—but is it biblical? I want to encourage you: not only does God *allow* us to take a few minutes to recharge, but self-care is actually essential to drawing near to God and being used by him. Look at the beautiful picture in Jeremiah 17:7–8:

> Blessed is the man who trusts in the LORD,
> whose trust is the LORD.
> He is like a tree planted by water,
> that sends out its roots by the stream,
> and does not fear when heat comes,
> for its leaves remain green,
> and is not anxious in the year of drought,
> for it does not cease to bear fruit.

This tree is sending out its roots. It has stationed itself near resources of rejuvenation. It is receiving nourishment so it can produce fruit, even in the dry season. It's stocking up for harder times. We too can be firmly rooted, fruitful trees—but only when we send out our roots.

The Details

How do you send out your roots? How do you receive nourishment and recharge your batteries?

Self-care will look different for every person, but it all starts on the inside with our relationship with God. If we seek satisfaction apart from Christ, we will always come up empty. We will be like the woman at the well who was always thirsty. Jesus looked at her and said, "If you knew the gift of God . . . you would have asked him, and he would have given you living water" (John 4:10).

Self-care starts with drinking deeply of that living water. We find it in the time we spend in prayer and in God's Word, and we also find it in our local church.

When we think of self-care as a way for us to serve others better, we don't have to feel guilty about it. We don't need to feel bad telling the kids, "You're going to play quietly on your beds while Mommy reads her Bible."

My five kids range in age from one to nine, and we have never stopped naptime. For the older ones, naptime simply evolved into quiet time. It's essential for me to recharge for a few minutes in the middle of the day. As soon as the little ones go down for their naps, the older ones go to their rooms to play quietly. I take a few minutes to eat lunch (without anyone asking for my food), check my email, watch a few minutes of a show, and catch up with a friend on social media. When I'm done, I feel like a new woman.

Self-care doesn't have to look super spiritual or holistic. Sometimes it means eating a brownie in peace and surfing Pinterest. The point is recharging ourselves for the sake of the work God has given us. Whatever refreshes you to be able to serve better deserves a place in your priorities.

Give Your Lists to God

Even just reading through these six categories reminds us of how many precious things God has entrusted us with. What a privilege! And what a responsibility.

Our goal, as we prioritize, is not to accomplish everything perfectly. Our goal is to use our resources to the best of our abilities and to leave the results in God's hands. Our hope is in Christ, not in perfectly planned priorities. We make our lists and then commit them to God. Our work is his. When we've done what we can, we can call it a day. We can say with David in Psalm 4:8, "In peace I will both lie down and sleep; for you alone, O Lord, make me dwell in safety."

What Other Moms Are Saying

Priority 4: Home

A tidy home is a ministry to my family and to others. But "tidy" doesn't always have to mean "deep cleaned." I allow my kids to play and make messes, but I teach them to clean them up. (Janet)

Whoever said "Many hands make light work" definitely didn't have children! Mummy cleans effectively when all the "many little hands" are asleep. I train them to clean—but I consider those training times, not actual cleaning times. (Hermine)

My husband and I both work. We've found that hiring someone to clean the house once a month helps us to focus on each other and the kids when we're home. It's a privilege we're thankful for. (Kristi)

Priority 5: Church

I encourage other moms to accept the season they are in. This might not be the time to do the same ministries at church that you did before you had kids—and that's okay. Look for ministries that your kids can do with you, like setting out the hymnals or folding bulletins. (Brenda)

Every month, my husband and I pick one family from church who we want to minister to, and we have them over for dinner. (Paris)

I can't tell you how many times I have felt drained physically or emotionally and haven't even wanted to go church or to Bible study—but I have always been so glad I did. There is something so refreshing about fellowshipping with other saints. (Andrea)

Priority 6: Self

I prioritize fueling my heart first, during down time, so that if naptime is shorter than expected or is interrupted, I'm ready to serve where I'm needed rather than begrudgingly doing so with a heart that isn't ready to. Practically, this looks like spending some time praying or listening to a podcast. We've recognized as a family that if I have an hour on Saturday to myself without the kids, that massively helps to reenergize me—and the kids look forward to that dad time, too. (Sarah)

Jesus is our example of how to recharge. He would slip away from the crowds in order to be with his Father. (Carrie)

Taking the time to grocery shop by myself, grab a coffee with a friend, go on a date with my husband, or just go shopping by myself for a few hours can be enough to recharge my batteries. (Danna)

Reflection

1. Read Matthew 6:34: "Therefore do not be anxious about tomorrow, for tomorrow will be anxious for itself. Sufficient for the day is its own trouble." How could this verse help to relieve your pressure when you feel anxious about priorities?

2. For each of the three categories we discussed in this chapter, identify its big-picture goal and one practical way you could achieve it.

Priority: **Home**

Big-picture goal:

How to achieve it:

Priority: **Church**

Big-picture goal:

How to achieve it:

Priority: **Self**

Big-picture goal:

How to achieve it:

5

Peace in Peer Pressure

If you look in the display cabinet in my kitchen, you will see some mismatched vintage serving ware, our homeschool globe of the world, and a framed sign that says, "Pardon the mess. My kids are making memories." That sign is my favorite thing in the cupboard. It's special to me because I had my two-year-old put his hands in paint and make handprints right below the words.

My husband always laughs at that sign and says, "It's so passive-aggressive. It says that you don't want to be judged for a messy house, so you subtly judge someone else for judging you for making memories. Before they've even judged you."

You know what? He's absolutely right. To me the sign says, "Yes, my house is messy, but it's for a *very* good reason." But the fine print says, "So if you were thinking about judging me, forget it. I wouldn't change the way my house looks even if I could. Now please watch where you step. I don't want you smashing any of my memories. Yes, including that empty juice box and the soiled burp cloth. You should feel honored to be here in my palace of priceless memories. You're welcome."

An exaggeration, yes. But it's a reminder of the little games we play as moms to make ourselves feel better. We feel like we have to have an excuse for everything. We have to justify every decision—not just for ourselves, or even for our husbands, but for other moms. We get caught up in the vicious cycle of comparing with and judging one another, all while doing everything we can to stay above judgment ourselves.

When I was little, a missionary came to speak at our church. During a Q&A session, someone asked him what the greatest challenge was that he faced as a missionary. We all expected something like language barriers or foreign diseases. His response was "Other missionaries." It was his own comrades who posed both the greatest encouragement and the greatest threat to his ministry at the same time. The jealousy and judgment from fellow missionaries were harder for him to deal with than any physical dangers he faced in a foreign country.

Sadly, we could often say the same about what our greatest challenge in motherhood is: other moms. We can't ever downplay the invaluable blessing of having other moms in our lives— but we know that Satan loves to work from the inside out. He would love to attack us from within our own circles.

When I had my first baby, I had trouble nursing him. I did everything I could possibly do before finally giving him formula. I felt like a failure. I had friends tell me that breastfeeding was natural, so if it wasn't working it must be because of something I was doing wrong. Every mom could nurse her baby, if she did it right.

One day I went to a friend's house with some other new moms. We all sat around the living room feeding our babies. I was the only one with a bottle. My husband and I had already decided this was the best decision for our baby, and if I had been sitting home alone in my baby's nursery I would have been okay with that. But sitting in a room full of nursing moms, I was not okay with it. I was the odd one out. I wasn't doing it "right."

We let anxiety creep in when we feel judged or criticized. It makes us question everything we do. We feel inadequate, inferior, and alone. In the age of social media, there is nowhere for us to hide. We can feel attacked in the comfort of our own homes, just by looking at our screens. It can be a help and an encouragement to read a blog about what another mom is up to, but if we're not careful we can get caught in the dangerous spiral of comparing. After scrolling through social media for ten minutes, I find myself thinking, *My kid's birthday party didn't look as good as* her *kid's. Why isn't her kitchen as messy as mine? Wait—she did crafts with her kids today* and *made that chicken pot pie?!* Just as there will always be another mom who does it better, there will probably always be someone who thinks that you're doing it "wrong." Judgment is a part of life. It doesn't go away when our kids get older. We have to learn how to process judgment through the lens of the gospel so that it makes us more like Christ instead of stealing our joy.

Who's Your Judge?

In chapter 1, we talked about our personal insecurities. We can hide our weaknesses from others (for a while), but we can't hide them from ourselves. We're a mess, and we know it. We saw that the solution isn't to downplay our weaknesses but to commit them to Christ. Since our new identity is grounded in Christ's righteousness, we don't have to make excuses anymore. We don't have to justify ourselves in our own eyes or in the eyes of other people. We have been justified once for all through faith in Christ, and now we have peace with God for all eternity (see Rom. 5:1).

My nine-year-old has been learning some hard lessons about injustice. His hot button is getting blamed for things, whether he did them or not. His brothers know it. If they really want to bug him, all they have to say is "It's your fault." He freaks out. He gets so angry and hurt. I can sympathize with him, because that's my first emotional reaction when I feel fingers pointing at me, too.

One day I pulled him aside in the middle of a meltdown. I shared with him what I'd been learning about how Jesus handled being treated unjustly. Instead of defending himself, Jesus "did not revile in return; when he suffered, he did not threaten, but continued entrusting himself to him who judges justly" (1 Peter 2:23). It was enough for Jesus that God knew the truth. This gave him peace. It took off all the pressure of having to defend himself. It took the pressure off my son, too. Later that day he told me he prayed that God would help him to be like Jesus instead of being defensive.

Imagine the very worst thing anyone could say about you. Maybe it's true; maybe it's not. Either way, you can confidently say with Paul, "Who shall bring any charge against God's elect? It is God who justifies" (Rom. 8:33). God is our judge, and he gets the final word. Our final word is Christ himself.

My dad has been a pastor for over thirty years. One day he was having a debate with a man who was trying to pin him down on the issue of sin. He wanted to expose the hypocrisy of Christianity and thereby destroy its credibility. My dad kept pointing him to Jesus until finally, in a fury, the man glared at him and said, "You're just hiding behind the cross."

My dad smiled at him warmly and said, "Yep."

Sister in Christ, we hide unashamedly behind the cross. We claim Jesus's righteousness for our own—not because we deserve it, but because God loved us when we were unlovable. We don't have to excuse our sin. We can call it what it is, because it has been paid for.

When you feel judged by others, remember who you are in Christ. You are clothed in his righteousness. You are not perfect, but you are forgiven. If you are a Christian, your judgment day has come and gone. God pronounced judgment on all your sin at the cross, and it will never be counted against you again.

Confidence in the Flesh vs. Confidence in Christ

It seems like every time my neighbors come over, we are having some kind of catastrophe. One time, a kind neighbor came by with fresh tomatoes from his garden. Just as he was handing them to me, my son came screaming down the hall, "MOM! Dad needs you! Somebody got hit in the face, and there's blood everywhere!" A few days later, a different neighbor came over to borrow my measuring spoons and almost got smacked in the face by a flying Bible. The kids were playing "Church," but the game switched to World War II and the Bibles suddenly became hand grenades.

With five boys, our family raises a lot of eyebrows. People don't know how to interpret the chaos—and I totally understand. But I also feel self-conscious. When the neighbors leave, I think, *Am I doing something wrong?* All my thoughts turn inward, and I feel a sudden urge to defend my parenting.

Unfortunately, when that uncomfortable feeling creeps in, I don't always turn to my identity in Christ. Instead I start making a mental list. I try to comfort myself with all the things I'm doing "right." It usually goes something like this: "Well, at least my kids were all dressed today. They all had baths within the last few days. Or week . . . I think. At least they were using a Bible . . . kind of . . ." If that doesn't get rid of the feeling, I switch to comparing. "At least they're not as wild as *some* peoples' kids.

At least they don't say bad words (yet). At least they are *happy* kids. They might be a little wild, but that's because I'm a *fun* mom." And on it goes.

It's ridiculous, because the list changes based on whatever type of judgment I feel. I want to be the fun mom, then the strict mom, then the cautious mom, then the informed mom, and so on. It's a list that never satisfies, because it's all about confidence in the flesh rather than confidence in Christ.

If anyone had reason to put confidence in the flesh, it was the apostle Paul. He did everything "right" among his peers. He was the most religious, zealous man of his day. He made list after list of his accomplishments. But in the end, the lists were empty. He looked at his lists of accomplishments and counted them as rubbish so that he could gain Christ. He knew that his righteousness could be found only in Christ (see Phil. 3:8–9).

We can't counteract the feeling of being judged by building ourselves up in the flesh. The only remedy for judgment is Christ.

How to Take Criticism

We've talked about all the wonderful, comforting reasons that we don't have to fear judgment from others. But what about the times when their judgment is right? God often uses criticism from others to help us grow and to show us our blind spots. Security in Christ helps us discern which comments to take to heart and which ones to discard. It allows us to respond to criticism humbly and confidently at the same time. When we feel judged, we can remind ourselves, "I don't have to let this destroy me, determine my worth, or dictate my decisions. But there might be some truth here that I can benefit from."

We can accept criticism, because we have nothing to lose. If the criticism is wrong, we set it aside and move on. If it's right, we admit it and ask God to help us change.

It's so much easier for us to take criticism when it's packaged nicely, isn't it? Earlier this week, a mom gave me suggestions on how to help my toddler sit still in church. I could hear the kindness and wisdom in her voice. I knew that she loved me and loved my kids. She wasn't telling me because she was annoyed; she genuinely wanted to be helpful.

Unfortunately, not all criticism is packaged nicely. We don't get to choose how criticism comes to us. We don't get to talk to other moms the way we talk to our toddlers and say, "Please try that again in a kind tone." Criticism comes the way it comes, and we have to decide how to respond.

Have you ever had someone say something to you about your parenting that was completely untrue? I have had things said about me that were just plain mean. My feelings were hurt. I had to fight the urge to comfort myself with confidence in the flesh. In those moments I prayed, "Lord, show me if there is any truth here that I can benefit from. And if there is not, help me not to give those comments a second thought."

God does not call you to be a doormat. You don't have to let someone beat you up emotionally for the sake of being humble. Maybe there is someone in your life who constantly criticizes you. Perhaps you even feel that their motives are unloving. If you've searched your heart and concluded there is nothing helpful in their criticism, give it to the Lord. Pray with David in Psalm 140:1–3,

> Deliver me, O LORD, from evil men;
>   preserve me from violent men,
>   who plan evil things in their heart
>   and stir up wars continually.

They make their tongue sharp as a serpent's,
and under their lips is the venom of asps.

Sometimes words are poisonous. We don't have to let poison into our hearts.

But what about when the criticism is true? How do we respond? I have learned that one of the worst ways to respond to true criticism is to ignore it. When a mom comes up to me in the park and tells me that my son is shoving bark down her son's shirt, I might be embarrassed, but I have to deal with it. Even if she tells me in an unkind way, I can't let my embarrassment stop me from doing the right thing. I have learned to say, "I am sorry. We are working on it." And then I deal with the situation. I also always try to say, "Thank you." That's my way of giving the other person the benefit of the doubt. It says, "You told me because you care, and your comments might benefit me." Even if neither of those things is true, "Thank you" helps me to diffuse my own pride.

The other day at lunch, my seven-year-old told my nine-year-old, "You have jam on your face." The nine-year-old just stared at him. He wasn't questioning the truth of the statement, but he stubbornly refused to do anything about it. He wanted it to be clear that he was not bothered by it. He put the jam there on purpose. There's no problem here. Move along.

I don't want to be like my son, standing there with jam on my face and saying, "I put it there." If something is brought to my attention, I need to be a big girl about it. If it's something that needs to be addressed, I shouldn't ignore it just to counter the embarrassment of being judged. I need to deal with it.

It's my confidence in Christ that allows me to deal with it. When I open my heart to accept criticism, I'm not accepting judgment that only God can give. I'm accepting criticism from another sinner, just like me, who might see something that I don't see. No matter the delivery, or even the validity, of that criticism, God is ultimately the one who is bringing it to my attention through that person.

The sanctification process is painful. God makes us more like Christ by knocking off our rough edges and refining our impurities. He often uses our brothers and sisters in Christ as his means of sanctifying us. The process might be unpleasant, but the end result is worth it. Proverbs 27:17 tells us that "iron sharpens iron, and one man sharpens another." I need my sisters in Christ to help sharpen me. I don't always like to be sharpened, but I do like to be sharp. I want to open myself up to God's refining process in my life, no matter how uncomfortable it is. And if it comes through a sister in Christ, I pray that my response to her will always be gratitude.

How to Give Criticism

Is it ever okay to tell another mom that she's doing something wrong? How do we do it? Unfortunately, our own sensitivity about being judged tends to create an unspoken rule: "You don't say anything about my parenting, and I won't say anything about yours." This might help us to protect one another's pride, but it doesn't help us to build one another up. We're afraid to offer criticism because it opens us up to criticism, too. But sometimes it's more loving to put our fears aside in order to help a sister in Christ. Let's take a look at four guidelines for offering criticism.

Consider how you can help before offering criticism. Play peek-a-boo with the screaming baby in front of you at the grocery store instead of telling the mom how to discipline. If a friend stumbles into church late, offer to hold her baby while she gets her other kids settled instead of telling her to get up earlier.

There are so many times that we raise our eyebrows instead of offering a hand. When you help, it tells the other mom, "I'm right here with you. We need each other."

Give criticism within the context of relationship. Have you ever had a total stranger criticize your parenting? Maybe your first thought was, *You don't know anything about me.* It's hard enough to take criticism, but it's even harder to take it from someone who doesn't know and love you.

Author Marissa Henley reminds us to evaluate our relationships with others before offering them help. "Knowing where you fall in your friend's network of friends can help you determine the type of support to provide. She needs your support, regardless of whether you are in her inner circle of closest friends, a middle circle of friends and close acquaintances, or the outer circle of acquaintances. But the way you will support her should vary depending on how close your friendship is."[1]

You might have something helpful to say—but are you the right person to say it? What kind of support is appropriate for your level of friendship? If your motive for constructive criticism is love, the most loving thing you can do is to build a friendship first. This will help you understand the right kind of support to give.

Offer constructive criticism for important *issues—not just your opinions.* Think of constructive criticism the way you think of tattling. I tell my kids, "Come and get me if there is blood, or if someone is hurting you and won't stop." If I saw my friend's child run into the street, I would grab the child and then immediately let my friend know. It's a matter of life or death.

But the truth is that these situations come up much less often than the situations that we usually want to judge. We usually want to judge based on personal opinions. "That's way too young for a cell phone. Her kids eat too much fast food. That family is involved in too many sports (or not enough sports)." But these are the criticisms we *don't* need to give. We need to acknowledge that God made every parent different—and thank goodness, because every *child* is different, too. I might think that I know what's best for my kid, but that doesn't automatically translate into knowing what's best for someone else's kid.

Give criticism the way you *want to receive criticism.* If I'm being totally honest, I don't ever like to hear negative things about my parenting or my kids. But it's so much easier to take when it's done in love. One time, a neighbor came to tell me that one of my sons had hit her son in the face with a plastic sword. I was so embarrassed, but she just laughed and said, "Well, now we're even. Remember when my son threw gravel at your kids last week?" We laughed together and shared the burden of raising little sinners. I did not feel judged by her. I felt her sympathy. At the same time, I was so glad that she told me because I was able to address it with my son. It was a good reminder to me that we as moms should share one another's burdens—not just point them out.

Receive Grace to Give Grace

Have you ever noticed that the more critical you are of others, the more critical you are of yourself, and vice versa? We judge others because *we* feel judged. And when we feel judged, we judge others more.

Giving grace to others starts with recognizing the grace that we ourselves have received in Jesus Christ. My dad once preached, in a sermon, "You can't give grace if you aren't receiving grace."

Sister in Christ, we have received a great grace. If you are not walking in that grace on a daily basis, you will not be able to give it to others. If you live your daily life as if God is a hard taskmaster, never pleased with what you do, and always disappointed in you, that is the lens through which you will see your fellow sisters.

But that is not our God. We have been adopted as his precious daughters (see Eph. 1:5). We are flawlessly beautiful in his sight (see Song 4:7). We are heirs of heaven and sharers of the very glory of Christ (see Rom. 8:17). Let these precious truths daily relieve your heart of judgment and doubt. Then we can smile at one another and say, "You are doing great! Hang in there, sister. We're all flawed, but God's grace is sufficient." Since we have freely received this grace, we can give it just as freely (see Matt. 10:8).

An encouraging word can set a mom free to be who God wants her to be. A critical word can trip her up and cause her to lose focus on what's truly important. Romans 14:13 says, "Therefore let us not pass judgment on one another any longer, but rather decide never to put a stumbling block or hindrance in the way of a brother." So let's decide right now. Let's decide to encourage instead of criticizing. Let's build up instead of tearing down. Let's drink deeply of God's grace so we can pour a refreshing drink for another weary mom.

What Other Moms Are Saying

I often have to tell myself, "Be good with being misunderstood." It's so hard to know that someone is judging you without having all the information or understanding where you're coming from. This saying helps me not to feel the need to explain myself, which is very freeing. (Autumn)

The more time I spend on social media, the more I tend to feel judged. I try to spend more time in real conversations. (Bekah)

When I feel judged, I take it back to Scripture. Maybe it's something God wants me to work on. But if it's based purely on opinions and not on Scripture, I let it go and move on. (Christy)

Find others who will pray for you. I have felt the weight of being judged by others lifted off my shoulders when I remember that I also have many wonderful friends who pray for me. (Christel)

I try to remember there is no way to compare myself to other moms, because not a single one of us is the same or has experienced the same things in the same way at the same time! So there's no accurate way to compare, and I have no grounds to judge. That is freeing to me. (Alex)

When I feel judged about my kids' behavior, I remember it is God who is ultimately working in their hearts. Sometimes I need to be patient. (Bekah)

God has brought me to the realization that it's impossible for me to meet everyone's expectations for me, and so the only one I need to worry about is God. As long as I am meeting his expectations, I simply don't worry about others. (Andrea)

I struggle with feeling criticized by older moms who don't remember the blatant sinfulness of toddlers and young kids. I get the feeling that they're thinking, "My kids never did that!" (Laura)

I feel at peace when I'm on the same page as my husband. If we are united in what we do for our kids, it doesn't really matter what other people say. (Heather)

Reflection

1. Read Paul's response to being judged in 1 Corinthians 4:3–4: "But with me it is a very small thing that I should be judged by you or by any human court. . . . It is the Lord who judges me." How does Paul's perspective encourage you?
2. Think of a time you felt hurt by someone's criticism. How does remembering who you are in Christ put that situation in perspective now?
3. How do you usually respond when you feel judged? Do you think your response reflects confidence in the flesh or confidence in Christ?
4. Pick a humble phrase you could use as your go-to response when you feel like someone is judging you. Write it here. (Examples would be "We are working on it" or "Thank you for the suggestion.")
5. Read Proverbs 12:18: "There is one whose rash words are like sword thrusts, but the tongue of the wise brings healing." Do you know another mom who could use a kind word? Write a prayer for her here and look for an opportunity to encourage her this week.

Part 2

Committing Your Children to God

6

Peace in Letting Go of Control

This afternoon I dove for my toddler, who was standing precariously on the edge of the couch. I grabbed him just in time—but I forgot that I had a watering can in my hand, and I dumped water all over him in the process. If motherhood makes you feel completely out of control, you are in good company. Motherhood turns everything upside down: our homes, our schedules, and our ability to predict what's going to happen next.

The mess. The noise. The unpredictability. Motherhood can be a rude awakening to how very little control we have over our lives and over the lives of our kids. It's the type of painful refining we don't usually ask God for—but he graciously gives it to us in order to drive us closer to himself.

This chapter isn't specifically for "control freaks." It's for any mom who has ever been caught off guard by the daily twists and turns of motherhood. Some women love control, while others would consider themselves pretty laid-back. But whether you're laid-back or a control freak, we all have expectations. We have all created some level of predictability in our lives—and kids throw it completely out of whack.

When Control Is Helpful

We usually associate control with power-tripping or manipulation. But control can also be a good thing. In the beginning of this book, we talked about the unique skill set God gave to us mothers to help us to care for our kids. Our desire for control is part of that. It's part of accepting the responsibility of being a mom. From the time our kids are born, we control absolutely everything in their lives: what they wear, what they eat, who they play with, what they play with, where they go, and where they sleep. And that's the way it should be. We are rising to the challenge that God put in front of us. He says, "Raise these kids." We say, "You got it"; and away we go, adjusting car seats and thermostats and reading food labels until we can't see straight.

When my kids are sick, I set my alarm to check on them in the middle of the night. I make my seven-year-old wear a very uncomfortable bathing cap in the pool to protect his ear tubes. I am constantly walking around our home analyzing their environment: Do they have enough room to play? Is there anything they could hurt themselves on? How can I help them thrive in this home? We are driven by love to protect our kids.

Control is a necessary part of our calling. God charged us with raising our children in the ways of the Lord (see Deut. 11:19). We are to protect them, nourish their minds and bodies, and help them to grow in the knowledge of God. We can't do any of that without some level of control.

Our desire for control also comes from God-given wisdom. We know what would happen to our kids if our control were removed. The Bible says that our kids are born sinners. They do not know right and wrong (see Prov. 22:15). We must teach them. They need our boundaries and our discipline. I control how big a scoop of ice cream my two-year-old gets, because if I handed him the whole bucket of ice cream he would eat it until he got sick. That would be *my* fault, not his. I am the one God has placed in authority. I'm the one with the badge that says "Parent." I will be responsible before God for how I raise my children.

We are the buffer between our kids and the world. From literal spoon-feeding to big-kid talks about friendship, whatever hits them goes through us. It's our job to teach our kids how to process everything they experience. I'll never forget my pastor saying, "If you don't catechize your kids, the world will." Something or someone is always influencing our kids. If it's not us, it's the world. We need to step up to the plate and accept this responsibility with confidence.

Our goal is not to hold on to the reins forever, but to let them out gradually, little by little. We want our kids to become independent, happy, productive members of society. That means controlling their environment and their choices when they're young. I don't let my toddler play in the street, because he wouldn't have time to learn from his mistake—his mistake could be deadly. But as our kids grow, we give them more choices. We look for ways to let them fall down and then pick themselves back up. Our control is a means to an end: freedom. In this sense, control is loving and beautiful. But there is a negative side to control, too.

When Control Is Hurtful

My uncle has a ventriloquist doll. It's one of the creepiest things I've ever seen. He likes to put it in different rooms of the house so that, when we visit, we never know when we might bump into "Howdy."

When I think of the word *control*, I often think of that puppet. This is also the way the non-Christian community usually views control. The world might say to us, "How dare you control your children? You just want power. You just want to feel good about yourself by manipulating someone weaker than you." We've already seen that our control can be a beautiful gift to our children, but it all depends on our motives. *Why* do we want to control our children? There are two motives that can cause us to misuse our control.

1. When It's All about Me

I'm an anxiety attack waiting to happen when I seek to use control for my own benefit. When I obsess over a clean house and well-behaved children because of how I want people to think of me, control brings misery to my family instead of blessing.

I think about a typical Sunday morning in the Wallace house. It starts out peacefully, but the stress gains momentum as neatly combed heads are mussed, shoes are lost and found and then lost again, and cereal is spilled on clean shirts. As the stress builds in my own heart, I'm not usually thinking about preparing for worship. I'm thinking about how our family will look when we finally come filing in. Will we be late? Will we look put together? Will I look like a good wife and mom or like the crazy person I feel like on the inside?

You know that this scene never ends well. It usually ends with hurt feelings, yelling, and anything but a feeling of being ready for worship. But when I put myself aside, my stress melts away. I'm able to prioritize the right things. Can we worship God with mismatched socks? Yes. Is it worth being late in order to thoughtfully discipline a disobedient child? Yes. My control then becomes about serving others rather than about myself.

2. When It Replaces Trust

My friend confided in me recently that she was a mess of anxiety. I was shocked, because you couldn't tell from the outside. She has her master's degree, she exercises every day, and her home is always organized. She has a definite plan for raising her three children, and she executes on that plan every day. She's not the kind of mom you would look at and think, "She needs help."

"It's because I keep trying to do everything in my own strength," she said. "But it's never enough. There's always something I didn't do quite right or something I left undone."

She went on to tell me a passage that was currently transforming her anxiety: "Trust in the LORD with all your heart, and do not lean on your own understanding. In all your ways acknowledge him, and he will make straight your paths" (Prov. 3:5–6).

My friend was leaning on her own understanding, just as I often do. She was replacing trust with control. Everything in her home and her parenting was going smoothly, so she stopped praying and reading her Bible. She was handling it. But the less she acknowledged God, the more anxious she became.

Imagine learning to drive a wagon that's being pulled by a herd of wild mustangs. (If you have boys, that's not hard to imagine—it's daily life.) The instructor hands you the reins and then puts his hands over yours. You are controlling the wagon, but your control is within someone else's control. No matter how you use the reins, you can feel the strong, capable hands over yours. Now imagine that you yank the reins away from the instructor and say, "I've got this." It might feel exhilarating for a few seconds, but when the wagon begins to swerve, you suddenly realize that you can't feel the security of those guiding hands. By seeking *more* control, you find that you are less in control than ever.

Thankfully, no matter how many mistakes we make, God

never removes his hands from his children—even if we try to push them away. But when we say, "I've got this" and turn our eyes away from him, we rob ourselves of peace and security.

Sometimes I look at my hands and wonder, "Are my white knuckles showing?" I can hold on to control so tightly that I'm almost sure it can be seen. That's when I have to loosen my grip, take a step back, and ask myself if I've been leaning on my own understanding. Am I leaning on my Google research? Am I leaning on technology and on developments in safety? Research and due diligence are good ways to be responsible parents, but they can also create anxiety. We are to *use* our research, resources, and gifts—but not to *rest* in them. This is a fine line. What does it look like practically?

When to Work, When to Rest

There is a constant tension between working and resting. When do we hold on to control, and when do we let go?

Sometimes the hardest thing to do is nothing. But there are times when God calls us to lay our control down at his feet and just be still. This happened to me a couple of years ago when one of my babies was sick. I thought I had to stare at him all night just in case something happened. My husband gently reminded me that that was unreasonable. That wouldn't help my baby, and it certainly wouldn't help the other children I had to tend to in the morning. He asked me, "Have you done everything that is reasonable?" I looked at my baby monitor, the humidifier, and the baby's medication. "Yes . . . ?" I answered hesitantly. "Then go to sleep," he said. "God is in control."

I thought I was trusting God by micromanaging the situation, but I was working when I should have been resting. I was holding on too tightly.

Being still makes us uncomfortable. We're afraid of what will happen if we don't *do* something. But I love that Psalm 46:10 tells us exactly what will happen if we are still before God: "Be still, and know that I am God. I will be exalted among the nations, I will be exalted in the earth!" God will be exalted. Period. He will accomplish his purposes.

I remember calling my mom in tears one day. I had just finished bath time, and the bathroom was flooded—again. Apparently there was no way my two toddlers could take a bath without emptying the entire tub onto the floor. I was angry that I could not get control of the situation. My mom said, "Have you thought about putting another towel down on the floor?" No, actually—I had not. I was so focused on controlling the situation itself, I had not even considered accepting the situation as it was and working within my limitations.

For some reason, the thought of laying down extra towels felt like defeat. I thought I was supposed to be so in control of the situation that I wouldn't need the towels. But those crazy expectations were creeping into every area of my life. For instance, "If I'm a good mom, my house won't be a mess. We'll never eat a burned dinner. I won't need help. My kids won't get sick or hurt." My expectations of how much control I would have were completely unreasonable.

For me, being still meant soggy bath towels. It meant letting go of the little things and focusing on what was important.

But here's the tension: If I let go completely, my entire house would be soggy. It would be total chaos. I'd be sitting on the couch with a pint of Häagen-Dazs ice cream, and the kids would be running around screaming and destroying things. We are supposed to work *and* rest. We usually think of this as a balancing act. We work a little and rest a little, back and forth all day. But it's not about doing equal amounts of work and rest;

it's about doing both at the same time. Sound impossible? Jesus showed us how work and rest go hand in hand when he said, "Take my yoke upon you, and learn from me, for I am gentle and lowly in heart, and you will find rest for your souls" (Matt. 11:29). A yoke represents work. And yet, when we do all our work for Christ and through his strength, it is a restful work.

As my husband and I carefully picked out ten boys' names (both first and middle names), "Jehoshaphat" never made the list. But King Jehoshaphat's experience in 2 Chronicles 20 is one of my absolute favorite stories in the Bible.

King Jehoshaphat got some bad news: a great multitude was coming after him. He gathered all of Judah together and cried out to God, saying, "We are powerless against this great horde that is coming against us. We do not know what to do, but our eyes are on you" (v. 12).

God gave a jaw-dropping response: "You will not need to fight in this battle. Stand firm, hold your position, and see the salvation of the LORD on your behalf" (v. 17). "The battle is not yours but God's" (v. 15).

God told Jehoshaphat probably the last thing he expected to hear: "*Don't fight.*" But he didn't tell Jehoshaphat to do nothing. He told him to do three things: *stand* firm, *hold* your position, and *see* the salvation of the Lord. The next day, the battlefield was covered with the dead bodies of his enemies—and Jehoshaphat's army never raised a sword.

Are you facing a battle you cannot fight? Maybe you don't know how to fight it, or you recognize that you are powerless against it. But there is something you can do: stand, hold, and see. Resting in God is not passive. It's a purposeful rest. We fix our eyes on him and go down to the battlefield. God did not tell King Jehoshaphat to stay in bed that day. He told him to go. He wanted Jehoshaphat to see his deliverance. When you feel that tension between doing and resting, remember that resting *is* doing. We rest expectantly. No matter what the battle is, it always belongs to the Lord. Sometimes we will be called to fight in it, and sometimes we will be called to watch and wait.

A Quiet Heart

In her book *Keep a Quiet Heart*, Elisabeth Elliot shows us how trust is the greatest simplifier of our lives. "Every assignment is measured and controlled for my eternal good. As I accept the given portion other options are cancelled. Decisions become much easier, directions clearer, and hence my heart becomes inexpressibly quieter."[1] Even the out-of-control moments are carefully measured by our loving heavenly Father. We are foolish to assume that just because we don't understand what's going on, God must not be in control.

Sometimes God has to painfully pry control out of our hands. But he removes control only so he can give us something better: himself. In those scary moments when we feel all control slipping away, we remember that we are standing on a sure foundation. We can tell our hearts, as David did, "For God alone, O my soul, wait in silence, for my hope is from him" (Ps. 62:5).

My sister told me that she had a strange visit with a friend last week. They were having a nice chat on the front porch when her friend glanced down at her phone and said to my sister, "Where is your husband?" My sister said, "He's at work. Why?"

"Could you call him?" her friend asked. Her voice was controlled, but shaky.

My sister, very confused, said, "Okay." She dialed her husband, and he picked up. As soon as her friend saw that he had answered the phone, she burst into tears. She showed my sister her phone—a notification said that someone with the same name as my sister's husband had been killed moments ago in a motorcycle accident in their town.

Relieved and shaken by the "what-ifs," my sister wondered why God had allowed this interruption to her otherwise very pleasant day. But instead of dwelling on the "what-ifs," she thanked God for another day with her husband. We don't know what will happen next, but we know who is in control.

My sister's experience was a reminder that a quiet heart doesn't come from controlling our circumstances. It comes from controlling our responses. Do we freak out at every reminder that we are not as in control as we think we are? If control is what ultimately gives us peace, then it's a false peace. Everything could change in a moment. That shouldn't scare us; it should cause us to look to who is really in control and to receive true peace.

My five little boys are continually teaching me that my attitude is sometimes the only thing I can control. Here's how:

What I Can't Control	What I Can
I can't stop the granola bar from getting ground into the carpet . . .	. . . but I can keep a "gentle and quiet spirit" (1 Peter 3:4).
I can't answer 167 questions . . .	. . . but I can give "a soft answer" (Prov. 15:1).
I can't predict when I will be wiping up barf . . .	. . . but I can "do all things without grumbling" (Phil. 2:14).
I can't accomplish everything on my to-do list . . .	. . . but I can be faithful in the little things (see Luke 16:10).

I can't get back the lost hours of sleep . . .	. . . but I can "pour [my]self out" for my family (Isa. 58:10).
I can't solve all my kids' problems . . .	. . . but I can trust in the Lord with all my heart (see Prov. 3:5–6).
I can't skip potty-training, sleep-training, or act-like-a-human training . . .	. . . but I can "work heartily, as for the Lord" (Col. 3:23).
I can't speed up or slow down this phase of life . . .	. . . but I can praise God that my times are in his hands (see Ps. 31:15).

I fool myself into thinking that my kids need a perfect home, a perfect diet, and a perfect education, when what they really need is a mom with a quiet heart. The end goal of all my control is ruined if I am constantly stressed and anxious. But if I have a quiet heart, it affects everyone's perspective. When my kids see a peaceful, composed mommy, chaos doesn't feel like chaos. It feels like an adventure—a chance for them to help out and contribute to the family peace.

God never intended for us to handle motherhood on our own. He knows that we need help, and his provisions are a perfect match for our needs. Charles Spurgeon said, "We have great demands, but Christ has great supplies. Between here and heaven, we may have greater wants than we have yet known. But all along the journey, every resting place is ready; provisions are laid up, good cheer is stored, and nothing has been overlooked."[2]

Do you feel that something in your life has been overlooked?

That things are not turning out the way you expected and that you can't seem to change it? Your resting place is ready. It's waiting for you right here and now in Jesus Christ. He has "great supplies" of grace, forgiveness, and peace. Remember that every detail of your life is in complete control—not your control, but the control of a Father who loves you and works all things for the good of his children (see Rom. 8:28). Open your hand to him. Trade the temporary peace of control for the eternal peace of trust in a loving Father.

What Other Moms Are Saying

My twins have special needs, so I have had to balance control in unique ways. Since I have to be ultra-controlling in certain areas, such as their diet and who can babysit them, I'm much more laid-back in other ways. They climb trees, jump off boulders, and run as fast as they want. I feel like their special needs give me perspective. (Erin)

Growing up, I thought that rest meant laziness. I carried this attitude with me into marriage and motherhood. I thought I had to constantly be working in order to be a good wife and mom. My pastor finally told me that I can't control my circumstances by refusing to take a break. I slowly began to give my to-do lists to Jesus and to rest in his perfect to-do list that was accomplished for me at the cross. (Kim)

One of my favorite phrases is "Hold your blessings with an open hand." This helps me to put control in perspective. I hold on to my kids, but with an open hand, trusting God's plans for their lives. (Samantha)

From the time they are very young, we should give our kids age-appropriate responsibility and freedom over their own little worlds. While you'll have your family standards, rules, and expectations, and while you'll give appropriate discipline when those are broken, seeking too much control over our kids brings misery to both us and them. (Carlee)

To me, taking control means taking away my kids' option of making a mistake when the cost is too high. For example, I control everything they eat because they have deadly food allergies. But I give them independence in other areas, such as playing outside by themselves. (Lauren)

Reflection

1. What makes you feel the most out of control in motherhood?
2. We feel strong when we feel in control. But where does Isaiah 30:15 say that our strength really comes from? "For thus said the Lord GOD, the Holy One of Israel, 'In returning and rest you shall be saved; in quietness and in trust shall be your strength.'"
3. What part of your attitude do you need to change in order to submit your control to God?
4. What part of your actions do you need to change in order to submit your control to God?
5. Choose a verse from the "What I Can Control / What I Can't" table and write it here. Pray that God will bring it to your mind and comfort you the next time you feel out of control.

7

Peace in Discipline

"I can't believe they are letting us take him home." I looked at the tiny bundle in the car seat next to me as my husband drove us the short distance home from the hospital. My heart ached. My new baby was so precious and so helpless. I didn't even know him yet, but I loved him desperately. I so badly wanted to do this whole mom thing right. But I would soon learn that "right" was a very fluid concept when it came to babies.

Every new experience in my motherhood was a learning curve. Just when I thought I had one stage figured out, my son would start a brand-new stage. The day he got into a regular eating and sleeping pattern, I was on cloud nine. I felt like the world finally made sense again. I was more secure, more confident—until he hit a sleep regression phase and I had to start all over again.

But as he grew, I learned there was so much more to motherhood than measuring milk and counting dirty diapers. I had a little soul to raise. This sweet, tiny body had a sweet, tiny heart. And if I thought that meeting physical needs was tricky, shepherding his heart would prove to be my greatest, most precious challenge of all.

Do you ever stop and think about the fact that you are raising souls? Our kids need our guidance and discipline as much as they need food and clothing.

But discipline is hard to measure. How do we know when they need it, what they need, and whether we're doing it right? We measure our success as parents by physical, visible results. If our babies are gaining weight, we know that we're feeding them well. If the toddler's rash is clearing up, we're treating it correctly. But discipline works from the inside out. We can't always see the effects of it. This creates anxiety and frustration—and the temptation to quit altogether.

But before you throw in the towel, let's remind ourselves what discipline is all about. Is it about simply controlling our kids or conforming them to a certain set of expectations from our church or society? If these are the goals of discipline, we have every reason to be anxious. We can't keep our kids from embarrassing us (believe me, I've tried), and we can't live up to other peoples' expectations. So *why* do we discipline? What's the goal, and is the goal even attainable?[1]

It's really a shame that the word *discipline* has such negative connotations. We associate it with anger, pain, and guilt. And this makes sense, because the *need* for discipline arises from something negative: sin. Our kids are born sinners, and they need our discipline to protect them from their own sinful hearts. But the *goal* of discipline is love. We see this reflected in our relationship with God, because he "disciplines the one he loves" (Heb. 12:6).

The word *discipline* itself means to teach. It's not a list of consequences (although consequences are part of it). It's a way to create teachable moments in everyday life.

Discipline is a beautiful gift to our children. It gives them safety and security. It imparts wisdom and drives out foolishness (see Prov. 22:15). It reminds them that they belong to us. When we look at it this way, discipline is not negative. It is difficult, but it produces something positive.

So let's address our anxiety over discipline by first stripping away the negativity. Discipline might be painful in the moment (for us and for our kids), "but later it yields the peaceful fruit of righteousness to those who have been trained by it" (Heb. 12:11). We can counteract each negative feeling about discipline with truth from God's Word.

Discipline Negatives	Discipline Positives
Pain	Protection: "Your rod and your staff, they comfort me" (Psalm 23:4).
Frustration	Peace: "Discipline . . . yields the peaceful fruit of righteousness" (Hebrews 12:11).
Doubt	Wisdom: "The rod and reproof give wisdom" (Proverbs 29:15).
Guilt	Joy: "Discipline your son, and . . . he will give delight to your heart" (Proverbs 29:17).
Exhaustion	Love: "He who loves [his son] is diligent to discipline him" (Proverbs 13:24).

The more I meditate on these positive truths, the less frustrated I am by discipline. I see the big picture more clearly. My anxiety over discipline fades when I put discipline in the context of love. I'm not trying to fix my kids' actions; I'm shepherding their hearts. That means that I might not see immediate change, and that's okay. I'm in this for the long haul.

Armed with truth from God's Word and a fresh perspective, let's take a look at two effects of discipline that cause us the most anxiety: doubt and frustration.

Doubt: "Am I Doing This Right?"

Have you ever had one of those "Aha!" moments in discipline? You know—the moment that makes it all worth it?

My friend had one of those sweet moments last week at her three-year-old daughter's gym class. She told her daughter to move on to the next station in order to give another child a turn, and her daughter refused. The stare-down began. My friend said, "You need to move now." Her daughter didn't budge. The mom of the other child, sensing the mounting tension, said, "How about if my daughter counts to ten and then your daughter can move?"

My friend's daughter looked at her mother triumphantly as if to say, "See? I get ten more seconds. I'll move when she's done counting." But my friend immediately recognized the need for discipline, not for compromise. She calmly said, "No, your daughter does not need to count. My daughter needs to obey." She looked at her daughter. Her daughter looked at her. Then she sighed and said, "Okay, Mom." She skipped along to the next station, and my friend's heart skipped a beat. She told me later that she wasn't sure exactly what she would have done if her daughter hadn't moved, but she was so glad that she stood her ground and required obedience. All the time she had invested in training her daughter led up to this important moment—and paid off.

I have to admit that those "Aha" moments don't happen for me as often as I would like. More often I am left asking myself, "Am I doing this right?"

I have realized that the times when I ask this question the most are when I'm focused on my kids' outward actions rather than on their hearts. When I focus on their actions, I want immediate results. I'm more likely to discipline out of selfish reasons, such as embarrassment, tiredness, or anger, than out of love. If I don't get the results I'm looking for, I doubt everything that I'm doing.

But when I focus on my kids' hearts, I don't have to wonder if I'm "doing it right." I can discipline in love and grace and can leave the results in God's hands. When I focus on their hearts, my own emotions are in check. I don't discipline in anger. I'm content to invest in long-term heart change, even if I can't see the results right now.

I also find myself doubting my discipline when I compartmentalize it to include only those moments when I'm doling out consequences. But discipline should be woven all throughout everyday life. It's part of our daily relationship with our kids. Discipline is about how we talk to one another, how we treat one another, and what kind of behavior we encourage all throughout the day. If I think about discipline only when my kids disobey, I'll be less prepared. I'll be caught off guard and say, "What do I do now?" But when discipline is woven all through the day, I feel more prepared to handle disobedience. It helps the kids and me to be all on the same page. It leaves no surprises.

Frustration: "This Isn't Working"

I love to cook. One of my favorite movies is *Julie and Julia*—the story of a young woman who aspires to cook like world-famous chef Julia Child. My favorite line in the movie is when young Julie says, "You know what I love about cooking? I love that after a day when nothing is sure . . . you can come home and absolutely know that if you add egg yolks to chocolate and sugar and milk, it will get thick. It's such a comfort."[2]

I love it when things work out exactly the way I expect. It doesn't just give me comfort; it gives me security. So when my kids don't automatically do exactly what I tell them to (and they don't—go figure), it shakes my security. I feel like I must be doing something wrong. Discipline is one of those areas through which God has humbled me over and over again. And I'm sure there's more humbling to come.

What do you do when you feel like you've followed the perfect "recipe" but your discipline still isn't working? You've read all the books and blogs, and your toddler still gets out of bed. Your son still hits. Your daughter still lies. What's going on?

As Christians, we know exactly what's going on. We have the inside scoop, because we know all about a little thing called *sin*. God's Word gives us the behind-the-scenes look at what's happening in our kids' hearts. The Bible tells us that the human heart is "deceitful above all things" (Jer. 17:9). Our kids inherit Adam's sin nature just by being born (see Rom. 5:12). And if we still aren't convinced about the sinfulness of our little angels, Proverbs tells us that "folly is bound up in the heart of a child" (Prov. 22:15).

Rather than expecting our kids to obey automatically, we should expect resistance. This is a battle—not *against* our kids, but *for* our kids. This means that our kids will resist our discipline, no matter how perfect our strategy is. The problem isn't necessarily our discipline. It's our kids' hearts. When they don't respond to our discipline, it doesn't mean that the discipline is not working. It means that this is war. We are fighting for our kids' hearts—and so is our enemy.

There is a special sigh given by moms who have *just* disciplined the toddler for hitting, only for him to do it again seconds later. You know the sigh. It's usually accompanied by a groan, eyes rolling up to the ceiling, and maybe even some teeth grinding.

And that's when our hearts cry, "This isn't working!" It must be time to throw out our discipline plan and try something completely different . . . right?

Before you go back to the drawing board and completely reinvent your discipline strategy (and read 3,471 blogs on the topic), ask yourself these four questions. Maybe you don't need a new sticker chart or new creative consequences. Maybe all you need is a new perspective.

Discipline Strategy Test

1. What's my motive?

It's embarrassing when your kid starts flopping like a fish on the floor of Walmart because you took a toy away—but avoiding embarrassment should not be our motivation for discipline. Neither should anger, frustration, or pressure from others. These motives blur our discernment. They make us more likely to discipline harshly. Our motive should be love. We can test our motives by asking ourselves, "Will this consequence help my child, or is it just an outlet for my frustration? Will this help him in the long run or just force him to change his actions right now?"

Another way you can test your motive is to take a moment to calm down before you discipline. You might find that this significantly changes your discipline strategy. But even if it doesn't, it will redirect your motive and impact your attitude.

2. Does this address the heart or (just) the actions?

Are you having regular talks with your kids about *why* we obey? If not, your discipline will stop at their actions. If your child rips a toy out of another child's hands and you demand that he gives it back, justice might be served—but have you shepherded his heart? Ask your child, "What would be the kind thing to do? How would you like to be treated?"

Addressing the heart doesn't mean skipping the consequences; it means explaining them. You might not explain every consequence every time for every situation (sometimes the consequence has to happen quickly in order for the child to connect it to the disobedience)—but it's a good idea to work discipline into daily conversation in order to give your kids a framework for the consequences they experience.

3. Am I frustrating my child?

Do your expectations match your children's developmental level? Are you disciplining them for childishness? If you spank a toddler for dropping a sippy cup, you will frustrate that child. Our discipline should empower our kids to change as they are able to, through love and encouragement. However, a lack of discipline is also frustrating to a child. Where are the boundaries? Where is the concern and care? Children will test boundaries to know whether they are cared for. If they don't sense the boundaries, they will not feel loved and secure.

4. Am I mimicking my heavenly Father?

How does God discipline us? Well, for starters, he *does* discipline us. If your discipline strategy is weak or nonexistent, you are not mimicking the love of our heavenly Father. His discipline, though, is always for our good. He "disciplines the one he loves" (Heb. 12:6). The result of God's discipline is that it drives us closer to him. Does your discipline point your kids to God? Does it inspire them to stand in awe of his love and holiness?

If you discipline your kids intentionally and lovingly (albeit imperfectly), you can leave the results in God's hands. Visible results are not the measure of your success. Heart change happens on the inside, one tiny step at a time.

Sowing and Reaping

My second labor experience was my worst. My son was eleven pounds, and he was sunny-side up. Going on hour twenty-five, I remember thinking, *This will never end. I will be in labor forever.* That was, of course, a ridiculous thought. But the pain made me lose perspective. I wanted to hold that sweet baby in my arms, but I couldn't see past the painful work in front of me. I wanted to reap, but I didn't want to sow.

That's often how I approach discipline, as well. I want the benefits of well-behaved kids, but I forget how much work it takes to get there. I get impatient when my discipline doesn't pay off right away. I teach my little ones all day long about kindness, self-control, and good manners. The next day, I wake up to find that I have to do it all over again. Where is the harvest? When do I get to see the fruits of my labor? When I get to the end of one row of soil, there's another one. And another and another. There is the promise of fruit—but some days all I can see is endless sowing.

A couple of months ago, I went to visit an old high-school friend. Her kids are all about five years older than mine. As I shuffled my hoard of boys into her house, I immediately noticed her kids' behavior. They smiled at my boys, took them by the hand, and lovingly let them play with all their toys. They answered their silly questions with patience and got them drinks of water. They entertained my kids while my friend and I talked. I asked her point-blank, "How did you do that?"

She smiled knowingly. "It takes a lot of work. It takes days and days of practice. But it pays off."

I saw in my friend a glimmer of hope for my future. Right now I am still on my hands and knees in the soil—planting, planting, planting. I'm disciplining for the same things day in and day out. I'm a broken record of godly character traits and gospel truth. My friend is still planting, too, but her crop is a few years farther along than mine. The little green shoots are dotting the soil, and every once in a while she stoops to pick the first sweet fruit of the harvest.

Lately I have been getting those glimpses of harvest in my own home. Yesterday my six-year-old knocked his little brother down and immediately helped him up again. He even apologized—on his own! Later I heard two brothers fighting, and before I could step in I heard the seven-year-old say, "You boys should make peace with each other. How can you show love to your brother?" I treasured that sweet fruit. But I knew it wasn't time to sit back and enjoy the harvest. Not yet. I still have much sowing to do.

We get ourselves into trouble with our discipline when we expect to reap during a season of sowing. Discipline catches us by surprise. We think, "Didn't I already teach you that? Didn't I *just* discipline you for that?" We're surprised by how hard it is. We're surprised by how sinful our kids are and how much work discipline really takes. We want to reap when it is still time to sow.

We also forget that sowing is a season and that every season has an end. If we put off disciplining now, soon it will be too late. Our kids won't learn to obey on their own. Obedience comes through the seeds of discipline, which are planted by faithful mamas who tirelessly tend to them. Sowing is slow. It's repetitive. It takes focus and intentionality. Yes, we will break a sweat. Yes, we will get dirt under our fingernails. But soon the days of planting will be over. Now is the time to roll up our sleeves and get our hands dirty. Don't give up. Discipline again and again and again. You aren't banging your head against a wall—you're planting seeds of eternal life.

What Other Moms Are Saying

Discipline in public is a real struggle. One friend carries around a portable time-out seat: a bathmat rolled up in her diaper bag. She pulls it out at friends' houses or at church, and she has an instant time-out spot. (Jessica)

I always have to remind myself that just because I can't see the results of my discipline today doesn't mean that it won't pay off in the future. (Ashley)

I am much more calm when I require immediate obedience. If I give my kids multiple chances to obey, it gives them multiple chances to disobey. That just gets me all worked up. (Rebecca)

Just as God is refining, training, and renewing us moms every day, so our children need refining and training every day. We are all works in progress. (Jodie)

Last week at Bible study, my toddler kept throwing toys at other kids. I had to keep getting up and down to discipline, and I hardly got to hear any of the study; but I felt a sense of accomplishment because I put in the time to discipline her and be consistent. I know it will pay off later. (Jessica)

I write down verses in my prayer journal that match specific things that my kids currently struggle with. I love praying Scripture over my kids, and it's so encouraging to look back in my journal months later and see how God answered those prayers. (Kim)

An older mom once told me that a whisper is often more effective than a shout. I always think of that when I start to get frustrated. (Julie)

My son's Sunday school teacher asked the kids what their moms do to show them they love them. My four-year-old said, "My mom disciplines me." Just when I thought I wasn't getting through. (Jessica)

Reflection

1. What is the biggest discipline issue you are facing with your kids right now?
2. Choose your favorite verse from the "Discipline Negatives / Discipline Positives" chart and write it here.
3. How does that verse help you think through the discipline issue that you wrote about in question 1?
4. Out of the four "Discipline Strategy Test" questions, which one do you struggle with the most and why?
5. How does the idea of sowing and reaping encourage you to persevere in discipline?

8

Peace in Our Kids' Physical Protection

We are human moms with human kids—and we care about their very human needs. It's strep throat season around here right now. I have spent the last two weeks taking the kids to the doctor, one at a time, as they graciously share their germs with one another. Trips to the doctor make for long days. We can't get anything else done on those days. I fall into bed exhausted with a huge checklist left unchecked. But I push away that nagging checklist and remind myself that the kids got what they needed, and that's what's most important.

Physical protection is a huge part of motherhood. It can easily become all-consuming. As we saw in the intro, "Wired for Worry," our concern for our children's well-being is a good thing. Their physical needs have been entrusted to us. "Can a woman forget her nursing child, that she should have no compassion on the son of her womb?" (Isa. 49:15). We were made to care. Unfortunately, it can be very hard for us moms to care without worrying.

God expects us to do what we can to protect our kids. Even if it means spending every day, for weeks on end, at the doctor's office. Maybe it means staying up late to research new recipes in order to protect your child from food allergies. But there comes a point when each one of us have to recognize our limitations. We do not have sovereign control over our kids' safety and well-being. But God does. And we must submit everything that we do for our kids to his control.

The most practical way we can submit our protective instincts to God is by saturating our motherhood with prayer. There will be many times when we reach the end of our strength, knowledge, and ability to protect our kids—but we can never reach the bottom of God's love and care. We are limited, but God is not. He is the one who is "able to do far more abundantly than all that we ask or think" (Eph. 3:20).

As we bring all our concerns to God in prayer—whether big or small, physical or spiritual—we must be willing to trust him with the answers to those prayers. God delights in giving us our daily bread, but we don't get to pick what that bread looks like. When I hold my toddler who is hot and crying with an ear infection, I pray that the pain will leave. I'm asking for bread from my Father. But I know that his definition of bread might be different from mine. It's like when my five-year-old asks for a cupcake right before dinner and I say no. He is too little to understand why. I can ask and ask and ask for health and safety for my kids, but I have to trust that God knows what they need. He knows how to use them (and me) for his glory. If more pain means more glory, only God can help me to accept that. He can also help me to praise him for it.

Caring vs. Idolizing

You know that special panic that rises in your chest when something doesn't feel quite right? That motherly instinct is what snaps us into action. But when do we cross over from caring for our children to idolizing them? Idolizing our kids means holding them with a closed fist. It produces stress and anxiety. But we can pour ourselves into caring for our kids without idolizing them. Caring without idolizing looks like:

- not being the helicopter mom—enjoying your kids and watching them enjoy life within reasonable bounds of protection.
- being less likely to judge other moms or to feel judged by them—being confident in your decisions for your kids' safety rather than constantly second-guessing them.
- recognizing that your kids' well-being is ultimately dependent on God—not you. This protects you from guilt over things you can't control and from the temptation to think of all the hypothetical things that could go wrong.

How do you know if you are idolizing your kids' health and safety? Look at the three guidelines listed above and turn them into questions to test yourself: Are you an anxious helicopter mom? Are you judgmental of other moms' decisions about health and safety (or defensive about your own decisions)? Do you constantly feel guilty when your kids are sick or hurt? We can all answer yes to some or all of these questions at any given moment of the day. This is when we turn our anxiety back over to God and say, "I trust you. I've done what I can in my limited strength with my limited knowledge and limited power. I leave the results in your hands."

Sometimes when I'm anxious about my kids' safety, I think about my ninety-five-year-old grandma. She raised her kids on baby formula and canned food. She drove them around before car seats were invented. She did the best she could with the resources that she had. And the generations after us will look at what we did as parents and say, "You did *what*??" We have nothing to lose from being as faithful as we can be, as long as we work with joy and leave the results to God.

Comfort for the "What-ifs"

When you become a mom, nobody warns you about a brand-new door that opens up in your brain. It's not a cute, Chip-and-Joanna-Gaines farmhouse door. It's a dark, foreboding door that you never walk through intentionally but that pulls you in anyway. It's the door of the "What-ifs." *What if I'm not cut out for this? What if I'm not doing this right? What if something goes wrong?*

One Thursday night in March of 2018, one of my what-ifs came true. My baby stopped breathing. I recognized the seizure immediately and called 911. My twenty-month-old son turned blue, and time stood still. "Hurry. Hurry," I heard myself saying into the phone.

I have walked this path before. Another one of my sons also had a febrile seizure at the same age. When babies' fevers spike too quickly, their little bodies can't handle it. Febrile seizures are terrifying, but in the end they are harmless. They indicate a serious infection, but the seizures themselves leave no lasting damage.

As my baby's breathing returned to normal and he lay limp on the couch, the paramedics walked me through what was next. We had to get him to the doctor right away to find out what was giving him such a high fever. Thirty minutes later we were sitting across from the doctor getting the results: strep throat. The infection set in so quickly that he didn't have any symptoms before the seizure hit. He got his medication, his fever calmed down, and we were soon back in our own home.

Once all five kids were tucked into bed and the house was quiet, I finally took my first breath of the evening. *This is it,* I thought. *Now I can fall apart.* There had been no time to process what was happening during the event. Now I was left alone with my own thoughts . . . and that dreaded door.

The first time we experienced a febrile seizure, I walked through the door of the what-ifs for days. What if he hadn't started breathing again? What if it had been more serious? What if . . . what if. . . . It was hard to be thankful for my healthy baby when I was suddenly struck by the fragility of life. Things could change so quickly. How could I enjoy my baby knowing that it could all end at any second? New worries took the place of what should have been joyful relief.

But this second febrile seizure was different for me. When it was all over, I saw two clear choices in front of me: have a meltdown and freak out about all the things that could have gone wrong, or praise God for keeping my baby safe that night. I could live through all the terrible scenarios that *hadn't* happened, or I could thank God for another day to enjoy my baby.

In Melissa Kruger's Bible study on Philippians, *In All Things,* she tells about a near-death experience she had. She walked away from a car accident that should have killed her. Her reaction to the event revolutionized my thinking on worry versus gratefulness. "When we know we've been rescued, we look at everything in a different light, don't we?" she writes. "I came home and hugged my husband and children a little tighter, ate my dinner with a deeper enjoyment, and experienced an overwhelming sense of gratitude. My thankfulness overflowed into joy, even in the most mundane of tasks."[1]

Wait. I thought that trials were supposed to sober us up. I thought that being anxious was just being realistic. Melissa's response shows the exact opposite. Close calls remind us that we are not in control—and that's a good thing. They remind us that this world is not our home—and that's a good thing. Close calls don't say to us, "Watch your back. God is ready to pull the rug out from under you at any moment." They say to us, "God is in control. You will walk through what he ordains for you to walk through—nothing more, nothing less. He is on the throne, and he is good."

Are the what-ifs stealing the joy from your motherhood today? My sister Rachel, in her article "A Surrender That Is Safe," says that we worry because we don't want to be surprised by pain. We buy the lie that "I need to worry in order to prepare myself for the future."[2]

When I laid my baby down after the events of that Thursday night, my heart was filled with joy. I looked at the door of the what-ifs, and I closed it. I felt a tremendous sense of gratitude in their place—as well as freedom to enjoy my son. I have no idea how long I will get to enjoy each one of my kids. But I do know that the what-ifs don't prepare me for trials in the future. They only rob me of joy in the present.

The only way to close the door to the what-ifs is to walk through the door of gratitude instead. Trade each what-if for a praise. Replace the unknowns with the knowns. Thank God for something that you *know* to be true. When what-ifs cloud my thinking, here are a few of my favorite truths to cling to:

- Everything could change in a moment, but I know that "Jesus Christ is the same yesterday and today and forever" (Heb. 13:8).
- I don't know what tomorrow holds, but "I know that my Redeemer lives, and at the last he will stand upon the earth" (Job 19:25).
- I cannot control the future, but I know that "in his hand

are the depths of the earth; the heights of the mountains are his also" (Ps. 95:4)

- I don't know how I will bear future trials, but I know that "he knows the way that I take; when he has tried me, I shall come out as gold" (Job 23:10).

Comfort in Painful Realities

Much of our anxiety is over things that haven't actually happened. It's produced only in our minds. But sometimes it does stem from real events. What do we do when our worries are not hypothetical—when we're walking through real pain and heartache? Where does our comfort come from?

If you've experienced a close call with your kids, you know how it feels to tuck them in at the end of the day and say, "That was close. At least everyone is safe and healthy." But sometimes we can't say that. Sometimes we walk through painful trials with our kids and they're not "okay." It gives us an amazing opportunity to push our hope past "At least . . ." and further and deeper into something much more real.

Before we suffer, our hope is pretty shallow. "At least I have milk I can use in my coffee, even though I'm out of half and half. Whew." Then a trial pushes us a little deeper. "At least I have AAA, even though I'm stranded on a busy highway. Whew." The more our comforts and securities are stripped away, the deeper we dig to cling to something real and important. "The earthquake destroyed our home, but at least the kids are okay." We tend to boil our "At leasts" down to health and loved ones—which are truly great blessings indeed. But sometimes God allows even those precious securities to be moved just out of our reach. And he teaches us a new depth of hope in the process.

My mom met Bev in college. They instantly bonded over

their involvement in Campus Crusade for Christ. They attended the same college Bible study, where they both met their husbands. Together they would embark on the exciting new adventure of raising families.

But Bev's journey soon took a very different turn from my mom's. In 1986 my mom and Bev both had babies. My mom gave birth to my sister—a healthy baby girl. Bev had a daughter, too—but something was wrong. Little Kristie was born with a rare muscle condition.

As Kristie grew, her family's life revolved around her. It had to. Bev and her husband Mike had to do things in order to protect Kristie that "normal" families didn't have to do. They had to forgo party invitations and regular outings, because even the smallest sickness was deadly to Kristie. Her weakened immune system could not protect her. Their money and time went to hospital stays instead of family vacations.

When Kristie was three years old, she caught an illness. Her body, weakened by her muscle condition, could not fight the illness. After five weeks in a coma, Kristie passed away. In a letter that Bev wrote to Kristie after she died, she said, "Dear Kristie, . . . Nearly daily you said, 'Some day I will walk.' 'Some day I will dance.' 'Some day I will fly like Peter Pan.' That some day is here, honey, and we are so happy for you."[3]

In her book for families of special-needs children, *A Never-Give-Up Heart*, Bev talks about a comment from another parent that she will never forget. When Kristie was born, another mom of a special-needs child told Bev, "This is hard, but it's not the end of the world." Bev said that that statement was not necessarily true. It was the end of "a certain kind of world—a world where everything is perfect and 'normal.' . . . It was the end of a certain kind of world that we had dreamed of. But there is another world, one that I would have never chosen, but that has proven to be . . . more fulfilling, meaningful, and in some ways, more wonderful, than any I would have ever imagined."[4]

There might come a time when our individual "worlds," as we know them, end. But that is not necessarily a bad thing. It does not mean that we are alone or abandoned. Whatever new world we find ourselves in, we can be confident that God created it for us. He created it for our good and his glory, and he will be with us. In the darkest days of caring for Kristie and then grieving for her, Bev learned a depth of grace that she had never known. God's strength and mercy sustained her when her hopes and dreams were destroyed. He did not take away the pain or the trial, but he showed her a new kind of beauty—the beauty of choosing joy.

Before Kristie passed away, Bev had another baby. He was a strong, healthy baby boy. A couple of years after Kristie passed away, Bev became pregnant again. "Finally," she thought. "God will bring me the healthy daughter I've always dreamed of." Not only was Bradley not a girl, but he was also not healthy. He had the same muscle condition as Kristie.

Bev and Mike got to enjoy eighteen years with their son before he joined his sister in heaven. In those years, Brad was often the strong one when his parents were weak. One day, reflecting on the concept of hope, Brad wrote, "Hope is very meaningful to me because it makes me optimistic and reminds me of my relationship with Christ, who is my salvation. . . . There is always hope no matter what happens."[5]

When I think about Bev and her children, I remember this hope. Although her kids' bodies were weak and crooked, their outlook on life was shaped by faith. Both Kristie and Brad couldn't wait to meet Jesus. They made everyone around them want to meet him, too.

It's a great reminder to me that my kids' earthly bodies are not going to last. Sin has taken its toll on all of creation, including our bodies. Psalm 103:15–16 says,

> As for man, his days are like grass;
> he flourishes like a flower of the field;
> for the wind passes over it, and it is gone,
> and its place knows it no more.

I read that passage as a teenager and was very depressed by it. But now that passage gives me great comfort. It reminds me not to hold on too tightly to things that I can't keep anyway. These are not the bodies we were meant to have. That means that you won't share endless, pain-free days with your kids here. But you might be worshipping with them for eternity, where God will "wipe away every tear from their eyes, and death shall be no more, neither shall there be mourning, nor crying, nor pain anymore" (Rev. 21:4). There is greater hope for us and our children than these earthly bodies can offer.

Maybe you are a mom reading this book who has lost a child. The emotional pain is physically palpable. A dear friend told me that her heart literally ached when she lost her baby. She also told me that, because the pain ran deep, it created a deep path for God's truth in her heart. And her most encouraging words to me, just a few years after her loss, were "Healing does come."

Healing will come at different times for different people and in different ways. If you are currently living with loss, or living with a special-needs child or a child battling an illness, you are not alone. God is "near to the brokenhearted and saves the crushed in spirit" (Ps. 34:18).

I love that I can read the same passage of Scripture hundreds of times and still see something new. Suffering often causes things to jump off the page that I didn't see before. During a particularly dark time in my life, I read Psalm 62 and saw a word that I hadn't noticed before: *alone*.

> For God *alone* my soul waits in silence;
>> from him comes my salvation.
> He *alone* is my rock and my salvation,
>> my fortress; I shall not be greatly shaken. (Ps. 62:1–2)

There is no other comfort that compares to God. There is no rock, no salvation, and no fortress apart from him. As much as I want to build my life around the safety of my kids, a comfortable house, my husband, and financial security, none of those things will hold me. Only God will hold me and keep me from being shaken. Suffering causes us to narrow down our hope to the only thing that stands.

What Other Moms Are Saying

I love meditating on the fact that God is eternal. I can pray for eternal results, such as salvation for my kids, in the midst of my time-bound efforts to feed them and clothe them. That thought is life-changing for me! (Laura)

Practically, I think it's so important to teach our kids who safe and unsafe strangers are. Teach them to identify store employees, police officers, or moms with young kids if they ever need help. (Janet)

When my son was three, he was diagnosed with sensory processing disorder and ADD. My biggest stress-relief in caring for him has been prayer, as well as listening to my motherhood instinct. God gave me that instinct, and I find that I care for my son best when I listen to it. (Theresa)

Trusting God with my kids' physical safety is part of teaching them how to be adults *before* they actually become adults! I have to let go a little and let them have freedoms, even if it is hard for me. (Mary Lee)

I talk openly with my seven-year-old about some of the dangers of this world. I remind her to stand by her faith because, no matter what, we have God with us. The fact that I can't protect her from everything is a chance for me to point her to Christ. (Christel)

I was a tomboy when I was little, and my parents let me do whatever my brothers were doing. I fell out of the tree in our backyard, and I crashed my bike straight into a parked car. When I start to feel overprotective, I remember that bumps and bruises are part of life. (Rachel)

Reflection

1. What does the difference between caring and idolizing look like for you personally?
2. Read the following passage. How do these verses give us perspective on placing our hope in our kids' physical safety? "Now hope that is seen is not hope. For who hopes for what he sees? But if we hope for what we do not see, we wait for it with patience" (Rom. 8:24–25).
3. First Peter 5:7 says, "[Cast] all your anxieties on him, because he cares for you." What is your greatest care right

now about your kids' well-being? Take a moment to cast that care onto the God who cares for you.

4. How would you encourage a brand-new mom who can't enjoy motherhood because she is so anxious about her child's safety?

5. Thankfulness can ease anxiety. Make a list of three things regarding your children that you can thank God for.

9

Peace over Our Kids' Salvation

One day, two of my boys and I were munching on peanut butter and jelly sandwiches and talking about life. The five-year-old, having a very sensitive conscience, was telling us how bad he feels whenever he tells lies. "I feel so sad inside," he said. His four-year-old brother looked at him and said, "When I lie, I feel great!"

My kids are at all different levels of spiritual awareness. I can see glimmers of God working in their hearts—and lots of sin at work, as well. That conversation was a reminder to me that all of my kids can grow up in the same home under the same teaching, and yet their hearts can still turn out very differently. Now, my four-year-old has a lot of growing to do, and hopefully his conscience will mature. But God is the one who has to work faith in my kids' hearts.

It seems pretty easy to "make" our kids follow God when they're young. Kids generally go along with whatever their parents do. When we show our kids how wonderful Jesus is, they believe us.

But as they grow, we realize more and more that we as their parents don't have the last word on this. God does. So what does all our work actually accomplish? And how do we fight our anxiety over our kids' hearts?

God's Sovereignty

I wish I could sit down for coffee with Hannah from the Bible. "Hannah, how did you do it?" I would ask. I would love to hear her describe her journey of trusting the Lord with her son Samuel—starting with the fact that she couldn't even conceive. When the Lord answered her prayers and gave her a baby, all seemed like a happy ending. But Hannah had a long road ahead. Her son's birth was just the beginning.

When Samuel was a young boy, Hannah committed him to the temple to be raised by the priest Eli. Happy ending yet? Not quite. You would think a young boy would have all the best examples, and the best education, in the house of God. But the other priests, Eli's sons, were godless men. "They did not know the LORD" (1 Sam. 2:12). They slept with women who came to serve in the temple, and they offered strange sacrifices rather than following God's laws. We know from 1 Samuel 2:29 that Eli was judged for his part in his sons' sin. Sure, he was a priest in the house of the Lord, but he wasn't a good father. Would you have peace about your son being raised in that environment?

I think I would ask Hannah, "Weren't you confused? I mean, first God gives you a miracle baby, and then you commit that baby back to him—only for him to be raised by worthless, immoral men." It seemed like Hannah did all the right things. She even gave up all those special years with her child to let him be raised away from her, in order to fulfill her vow to God. Did God let her down?

Hannah's prayer after the birth of Samuel reveals a deep grasp on God's sovereignty. She didn't say what we might have expected a woman in her position to say, which is "God is good because he gave me a baby! Now everything will be all right." Instead, as she held the sweet little answer to prayer in her arms, she said some surprising words:

> The LORD kills and brings to life;
>> he brings down to Sheol and raises up.
> The LORD makes poor and makes rich;
>> he brings low and he exalts.
>
> . . . .
> For the pillars of the earth are the LORD's,
>> and on them he has set the world. (1 Sam. 2:6–8)

Basically, Hannah's response to her answered prayer was "God does what he wants. Praise the Lord." In her prayer, Hannah worshipped the Giver, not the gift. She didn't assume that since God had given her a baby, he now *owed* her the right to control every detail of that baby's life. Hannah knew that she was not in control. And she praised God for it. She might not have known it at the time, but that grasp on God's sovereignty would hold Hannah's heart through many uncertain days.

C. S. Lewis's wife Helen passed away just four years into their marriage. After her death he was tortured by questions: What was the point of it all? What was he supposed to learn from this grief? Why had God given him a wife at all? In *A Grief Observed*, Lewis wrote, "When I lay these questions before God I get no answer. But a rather special sort of 'No answer.' It is not the locked door. It is more like a silent, certainly not uncompassionate, gaze. As though he shook his head not in refusal but waiving the question. Like, 'Peace, child; you don't understand.'"[1]

Is it possible that we can have questions that God cannot

answer? Yes. Sometimes our grief and anxiety create questions that are not really questions. Lewis says it's like asking, "How many hours are there in a mile?" or "Is yellow square or round?"[2] But God does not slam the door in our faces. Instead he diverts our gaze away from our questions and onto his character. The foundation of our trust rests on God's character, not on our answered questions.

I want to look at my kids the way Hannah looked at Samuel and say, "God brought this child to me. I can trust him with whatever he does with him." It's easy to hold a newborn and acknowledge God's powerful hand. It's harder to watch that child grow up, make poor choices, and harden his heart, and still acknowledge that God is in control of every detail. But just as he was sovereign over every cell that came together in the womb (without any ounce of help from me), he is just as in control of every step that my kids take in this life. We can trust that God has a plan for our kids before they are even born (see Rom. 9:11). The ultimate outcome of our kids' lives depends not on our work or their work "but on God, who has mercy" (Rom. 9:16).

We can take great joy in the fact that God uses moms. Paul acknowledged that Timothy's faith was a direct result of the "faith that dwelt first in your grandmother Lois and your mother Eunice and now, I am sure, dwells in you as well" (2 Tim. 1:5). So if God is sovereign over our kids' hearts, where exactly do we come in?

Women of Faith—and Action

Abigail, Sarah, and Esther were all married to men who made some pretty big mistakes. But these women also had something else in common: fear of God. We see a common thread of faith in these women's stories. Sometimes the faith looked like waiting on God. Sometimes it looked like jumping into action. As we consider how God uses us as mothers, let's take a look at how these women put their faith into action.

Abigail trusted God by acting. When her evil husband Nabal offended David, Abigail's whole family was in trouble. But she was a woman of discernment and beauty (see 1 Sam. 25:3), and she had a plan. She snapped into action. I love picturing the scene in my mind: servants flying around preparing sheep, hundreds of loaves of bread, clusters of raisins, and fig cakes; donkeys being loaded with the gifts and led down a secret valley between the mountains—all while Nabal is completely oblivious to the danger. Finally, with Abigail at the helm, the whole company intercepts David and his men in the valley. Abigail falls on her face before David and pleads on behalf of her people. Her wisdom wins David and spares her entire family from his revenge. David praises her by saying, "Blessed be your discretion, and blessed be you, who have kept me this day from bloodguilt. . . . Go up in peace to your house" (1 Sam. 25:33, 35).

Esther also put her trust in God to work. A Jewish orphan who was raised by her cousin, Esther suddenly found herself in a strategic position in the king's household. She was the ultimate party planner. The feasts that she arranged with the king would change the course of history for the Jews. Each feast carefully built on the next until Esther had the heart of the king in her hands—taking her own life in her hands at the same time. Through her wisdom, the king's heart was moved to say, "What is it, Queen Esther? . . . It shall be given you, even to the half of my kingdom" (Esther 5:3). Esther asked for protection for her people—and got a greater deliverance than she could ever have imagined.

Sarah's trust looked more like quiet submission than action. She went along with some pretty crazy schemes from her husband, including pretending to be his sister (twice!). But in 1 Peter we get a glimpse into Sarah's heart. Her submission was more than just "going along" with Abraham. Her hope wasn't in Abraham. It was in God. That's why Sarah could follow her husband "without being frightened by any fear" (1 Peter 3:6 NASB). Her submission to her imperfect husband was a picture of her hope in a perfect God. Abraham might have made mistakes, but God never does.

What does all this have to do with trusting God with our children? When it comes to our kids' hearts, we have to know when to act and when to wait. We must remember that only God can change hearts, but that he has chosen to use moms as part of the process. This helps us to make a dramatic shift in our thinking. Instead of thinking, "I'm going to change my child's heart," we can think, "I'm going to be used by God in my child's life."

Have you ever prayed for someone, over and over and over, and not seen any change? I can think of unsaved people I've prayed for, for years, and who still aren't saved. The other day I was driving and praying for one of those people. It struck me that, as I prayed for this person, I was thinking, *I can't imagine this person ever coming to know the Lord.* It seemed like a miracle that was too big even for God.

It's easy for me to trust that God will make the sun rise in the morning. It's harder for me to trust that he can change someone's heart. But it shouldn't be. If I can believe that God sets an exact boundary for every ocean wave and knows the name of every star in the sky, then I can believe that "the king's heart is a stream of water in the hand of the LORD; he turns it wherever he will" (Prov. 21:1). He is the God who changes hearts.

This gives us great hope and encourages us to never give up praying for our children. No matter how little evidence of faith we might see in them now, or how far we might watch them stray, there is always hope.

Monica was a mother who tenaciously held to hope for her wayward son. Augustine is known as one of the greatest theologians of the first thousand years of church history. His impact on the spread of Christianity is immeasurable. But in his younger years, Augustine was far from God. He prided himself on human logic rather than the Word of God and indulged in an immoral lifestyle. Monica followed him from Africa to Europe, pleading with him to turn to God. She cried out to God to save her son. Monica got to see God answer her prayers, but only at the very end of her life. She spent a few special years rejoicing with her son in their shared love for Christ before she passed away.

We might not chase our kids from continent to continent like Monica did, but our prayers can follow them anywhere. What do the effective prayers of a mother look like?

My Prayer Problem

It's true. I have a prayer problem. Instead of letting prayer draw me closer to God, sometimes I let it take me down winding paths of worry. "Let's see. What should I pray about for my kids? Well, let's start with all the things that *could* go wrong. That sounds logical." Like the disciple Peter, I start to focus on the waves instead of on the Savior—waves, I might add, that haven't even happened yet and probably never will.

Last night I opened my prayer journal and saw five sweet faces staring up at me from the pages. I had taped a photo of each child in the journal so that I could look at them when I prayed. As I began to pray, I found that my sister was fresh on my mind. In 2015 she went through a devastating divorce. She has been writing about her experience and God's faithfulness.

As I looked into the innocent eyes of my children, I thought about my sister's pain. I thought about what trials God was preparing for my own kids. Would he spare *them* from the tragedy of a broken marriage? What about physical pain—would he keep them from harm?

But then I thought about the entire reason that my sister chose to write about her story. She wasn't giving five easy steps to avoid pain in your life. It was just the opposite. She wanted to show the unparalleled beauty of a faith that's refined *through* trials. "Don't be afraid that being used by God will mean future pain," she writes. "Of course it will. And hallelujah."[3]

I looked at my children. Used by God? I knew there was nothing I wanted more in this world than for them to walk with the Savior and be used by him for his glory. But I could not pray for that and pray that he would spare them from all earthly pain at the same time. Why not? Because pain and trials are a promise from God to all believers: "In this you greatly rejoice, even though now for a little while, if necessary, you have been distressed by various trials" (1 Peter 1:6 NASB).

In fact, Christians should consider trials normal. They should "not be surprised at the fiery trial when it comes upon you to test you, as though something strange were happening to you" (1 Peter 4:12).

Even more than I want my kids to have a pain-free life, I want them to be like Christ. I want the whole package. I don't just want "fire insurance" so that they go to heaven. I want them to have sweet communion with their Savior every day—to experience more than the superficial comforts this world offers. I want them to know their Maker. I want them to make an impact for the gospel in this world.

That means going through a refinement process. Refinement means fire. Fire means pain. It means that they will spend every day of their lives fighting against their own flesh and against the world. They will be ridiculed. They will groan with aching bodies for their heavenly home. They will have earthly comforts taken from them by a loving hand that wants to give them so much more. He will do this so that the proof of their faith, "being more precious than gold which is perishable, even though tested by fire, may be found to result in praise and glory and honor at the revelation of Jesus Christ" (1 Peter 1:7 NASB).

If this is what it means to be a follower of Christ, this is what I want for my kids. Does that mean I should pray that they experience pain? No—but I should be praying every day that God will draw them to himself and make them like his Son, even if that means trials. And it will.

Remember my prayer problem? I've found that I can solve it instantly when I bring my requests to God from the standpoint of what I already know about him. Instead of getting caught up in all the hypotheticals, it helps me to pray for what I *don't* know in the context of what I *do* know:

- I *don't* know that my child will never experience a heart-breaking loss. I *do* know that God "heals the broken-hearted and binds up their wounds" (Ps. 147:3).
- I *don't* know that my child will get a good job and be financially stable all his life. I *do* know that God "is a shield for all those who take refuge in him" (Ps. 18:30).
- I *don't* know that my child will avoid every devastating disease. I *do* know that "they who wait for the LORD shall renew their strength; they shall mount up with wings like eagles" (Isa. 40:31).

We never seek pain for our children. But when we put on our gospel-centered glasses, we can pray for things that are so much greater than earthly comfort. We begin to pray for God not simply to prevent every hardship that could come their way but to use it for their good and his glory.

Ten Days of Prayer for Your Children

There are so many wonderful things that we could (and should) pray for our kids. But nothing compares to praying for their salvation. And, since "the prayer of a righteous person has great power as it is working" (James 5:16), we mamas have some *work* to do. Our kids are too young to even know what their greatest need is. We need to cry out to God on their behalf.

"God, save my child." No matter how beautiful this request is, I can pray it only so many times before it starts to feel rote. I've compiled a list of "Ten Salvation Verses" I can pray over my kids in order to keep my mind and heart engaged in what I'm praying for. I love using Scripture in my prayers, because I'm literally praying God's own words back to him.

Here is a ten-day prayer challenge for you. Take a verse each day, for ten days, and pray it back to God, inserting your child's name. If you have a few kids, insert each child's name separately. Chew on the picture of salvation that each passage presents. Let the illustrations sink into your heart. And then tell your kids what you are praying for them! Let these passages encourage your heart and give you fresh passion for praying for your kids' salvation.

Dear heavenly Father . . .

1. Give my child eternal life so that no one can snatch him out of your hand (John 10:28).

2. Let my child hear your voice and recognize it as the voice of his shepherd (John 10:27).

3. Remove my child's heart of stone and give him a heart of flesh. Put a new spirit within him (Ezek. 36:26).

4. Make my child's heart good soil that will take in the seed and produce grain, a hundredfold (Matt. 13:8).

5. Cause my child to acknowledge Christ before men so that Christ will acknowledge my child before you (Matt. 10:32).

6. Make my child a good and faithful servant who will hear the words "Enter into the joy of your Master" (Matt. 25:23).

7. Draw my child to yourself and raise him up on the last day (John 6:44).

8. Call my child to yourself. Justify him, sanctify him, and glorify him (Rom. 8:30).

9. Give my child the gift of faith, which he could never earn on his own (Eph. 2:8).

10. Write my child's name in the Lamb's book of life (Rev. 21:27).

When we feel anxious about our kids' salvation, we must remember that salvation is supernatural. We can't make it happen. But God can. That gives us great confidence to pour the gospel into our kids every day, knowing that God can and will use weak vessels like us to accomplish supernatural things.

What Other Moms Are Saying

My friend's daughter walked away from the Lord and continues to live an ungodly lifestyle. I can see the physical and emotional toll it has taken on my friend—but she never gives up praying for her. She trusts God and is thankful for his love and goodness, even in the midst of such a painful trial. (Jessie)

One of my greatest joys in watching my babies grow into big kids is seeing their interest in spiritual things. Just an encouragement to moms who are still in the baby stage. (Janna)

I'm seeking to raise godly children while being married to an unbeliever. I take them to church by myself and teach Sunday school, and I created a MOPS group at my church. I pray for my husband all the time, but I never push. I know that God can work in both my husband and my kids. (Theresa)

When I'm anxious, I remember this: it is for us to say, "I need thee every hour"; it is for God to say, "I Am." It's amazing to think that he doesn't need me, and yet he loves me for no other reason than the "good pleasure of his will" (Eph. 1:5 KJV). What a God! (Andrea)

When I think about my kids' salvation, I remember God's omnipotence—nothing is impossible with him! He is capable of far more than we could ask or imagine (see Eph. 3:20). (Carrie)

It transformed my prayer life when I wrestled with the fact that God is unchanging. When I struggle with people who I think will never change, I am attributing something to them that is true only of God. God himself is unchanging—but he can change anyone. What a comfort! (Kim)

Reflection

1. Are you a "fixer" or more of a "watch and wait"-type mom? How does this impact the way you address spiritual issues in your kids? How does this impact the way you trust God with your kids?
2. Our kids are spiritual beings. What glimmers of spiritual awareness have you seen in your kids most recently? (If your kids are older, what comments or conversations about spiritual things have stood out to you the most lately?)
3. As our kids grow, our prayers often take on a more spiritual emphasis for our kids. What are some specific things you are praying for your kids spiritually right now?
4. Read Philippians 2:12–13: "Work out your own salvation with fear and trembling, for it is God who works in you, both to will and to work for his good pleasure." How does this passage help us to balance shepherding our kids' hearts with committing their hearts to God at the same time?
5. How does God's character shape your prayers? If you haven't thought about it before now, how do you think his character can shape your prayers moving forward?

10

Peace in Preparing Our Kids for the World

My husband got a very special present from his parents when he turned eighteen: the boot. It was time for him to leave the nest and venture out on his own. His mom took him to look at apartments, and his dad had spent many years leading up to that day teaching him how to be self-sufficient. He was on his own—but he knew he could go to them for anything, anytime.

As loud and crazy as my house gets with five little boys, I don't relish the day they will leave. Sometimes I cuddle the baby and whisper, "You can stay with me forever." If my husband overhears me, he says, "Oh, no he can't!" So I whisper to the baby that I will make him a special room in the basement.

But I know in my heart that I am not raising them to live in the basement. I am raising them to be independent, godly leaders of their own homes, churches, and communities. My only reservation is . . . the basement seems so much safer. How can I keep them safe and prepare them to leave the nest at the same time? How can I put my worry to work so that I equip them instead of smothering them?

Is "Sheltering" a Bad Thing?

When I was in sixth grade, my best friend called me a horrible word. She called me "sheltered." I was hurt—though I didn't know why. I just knew that it was a bad thing. I knew that it separated me from my friends and made them look down on me.

But it turned out that my friend had a strange definition for that word. She wasn't wrong that I was sheltered (as most homeschooled pastors' kids are), but she was wrong about what "sheltered" meant. Her reasoning went like this: "You don't know all the sinful things that go on in the world, therefore you are naive, therefore you are stupid." That's what *sheltered* meant to my friends.

As a mom now myself, I have to laugh at this reasoning. It makes it seem as if there are only two choices: either I can expose my kids to all the evils of the world or I can raise them to be stupid. Thankfully, those are *not* our only two options.

The other option is to *equip* our kids for the world. We can't keep them sheltered in our homes forever, and we also shouldn't let them experience every harmful, evil thing in the world. But we can use this short time that they are in our care to prepare them for the world. Preparing them for the world starts with sheltering.

I went straight from being homeschooled to attending a Christian college to getting married. My career was also in a Christian environment, as a Christian schoolteacher. I never really got "out" into the world (except for a few eye-opening business trips to Las Vegas with my husband). So now here I am, raising my kids and wondering whether I should be doing anything differently.

I recently asked a group of Christian friends if they considered themselves to have been "sheltered" as kids and how, or if, this had hindered them in any way. I was expecting some negative responses, but their responses were overwhelmingly positive: They were all happy their parents had sheltered them in the ways they had, and they didn't have any problems adjusting to the world.

But the key point each friend made was that their parents had *used* this time of sheltering to equip them. It wasn't sheltering for sheltering's sake. Perhaps you or someone you know has experienced painful consequences from being too sheltered. That can happen when sheltering is rooted in fear, pride, or a power trip. Many parents think they're doing the most loving thing for their children by sheltering them, but they take it too far. Good sheltering is purposeful; it's done for the sake of preparing our kids to one day leave home and be successful in the world. Good sheltering accepts the reality that the world is dangerous but believes that our children can still thrive in it.

What about those who weren't sheltered at all? Many people were raised with a more "hands-off" approach. When done intentionally and strategically, this can help children become confident and independent. But, just as with a hands-on approach, a hands-off approach can become unbalanced. In extreme situations, kids in "unsheltered" homes run the risk of being exposed to more of the world than they are prepared to deal with. They might even feel like their parents are indifferent about what they do or don't do. This can lead to a strained parent/child relationship. Parents who grew up in extreme "unsheltered" environments themselves are often driven to protect their kids from these same negative effects. The temptation is to counteract extreme "unsheltering" with extreme sheltering. But neither extreme will prepare our kids to thrive in this world.

When we feel driven to protect our kids from the world, we have to remind ourselves that such protection is only temporary.

One day they will face the world. Will they be ready? Thankfully, God has given us tools to prepare them.

The Greenhouse Effect

I don't know much about growing plants, but I sure know how to kill them—especially when I start with seeds. Inevitably I either forget to water them or don't use the right kind of soil. Either way, my poor kids have yet to taste any produce grown by Mom. And they probably never will. I'm okay with that.

Maybe if I had a greenhouse I would be a better gardener. The greenhouse provides the perfect amount of light, the perfect temperature, and protection from critters. It's an environment that vulnerable little seedlings can thrive in. As the plants grow, they eventually become ready to be transplanted so they will have more room to grow and spread their roots.

Right now my kids are seedlings. They are weak and vulnerable. They don't know how to care for themselves. They are completely oblivious to most of the things that can hurt them. They need my greenhouse so they can thrive in a worry-free, threat-free environment. It's my job to protect them. If I opened up the greenhouse and let them experience life for themselves, their growth would be hindered.

What does this look like exactly? One mom's version of protection might look very different from another's. And that's okay. That's why we don't have to make hard-and-fast rules about what the "right" age is for certain movies or whether or not our kids should dress up for Halloween. There is no rule about homeschooling vs. public or private school. There is no rule about moms who stay home or moms who work. Each mom is able to offer protection for her kids in her own unique situation. Protecting or "sheltering" our kids is not about fitting one particular mold. It's about creating an environment in which our kids can grow and learn about the God who made them.

I have a friend whose "greenhouse" is very limited. She has only a few days a week to protect and shelter her kids. The rest of the week they are at her ex-husband's house. He is a non-Christian who lives with his male partner. Her kids are exposed to much more of the world than she would have chosen—and at a much younger age. They are asking questions that she did not anticipate dealing with at such young ages. Can she still have a greenhouse effect? Can she still create an environment in which to nurture her children? The answer is yes. She can.

Maybe your greenhouse isn't the way you envisioned it, either. It creates great anxiety in our hearts when we feel like we can't give our kids the ideal greenhouse.

I want to encourage you with the reminder that the greenhouse you have is from God. He made it. It might not be what *you* would have created for your kids, but it is God's plan for them. He is in control of every detail. And even though there are days when you feel helpless, you never actually are. You can always use your abilities to pour into your kids. Whatever limited time you have with them—whether due to illness, a broken home, or circumstances beyond your control—be faithful. The resources you have are from your heavenly Father. Pray over your kids. Talk to them. Make special time to soak them up and let them feel God's love for them flowing through you. And don't despair. God is the gardener, and he knows each and every seed.

True Equipping

I have a couple of readers in the house now. My oldest two sons will grab anything with words on it and read it to me. Recently they've been reaching for the newspaper. I was impressed when my third grader read to me the latest news on the economy. Very educational, I thought. But I quickly remembered that the newspaper isn't rated G. The same page with the article about the economy had articles about a public official's affair and a sex-trafficking bust. Time to put the paper away for a little longer.

When I see a newspaper page like that in the hands of my sweet, innocent son, I get angry. I feel like my kids don't deserve to grow up in such an evil world. I want to protect them from everything "out there."

But the Bible says sin doesn't come from "out there." Sin comes from within. "For out of the heart come evil thoughts, murder, adultery, sexual immorality, theft, false witness, slander" (Matt. 15:19). Not from the newspaper. Not from the politicians. Not from the internet. Sin comes from the heart.

The best way I can prepare my kids for everything "out there" is to prepare them for what's inside their own hearts. Standing strong in the face of evil starts from the inside out. Right now, I can protect them from seeing pornography or hearing foul language, but as soon as they leave my house, I can't. Their decision to stand strong has to come from the inside.

This should instantly relieve our anxiety. We can't protect our kids from the world forever, but there is something we *can* do: we can give them the right tools. This is how we turn our worry into work. Let's get busy and start equipping our kids instead of worrying about them.

When I was pregnant with my third boy, I went to a women's Bible study at which we went through the book of Proverbs. I immediately started underlining verses that I wanted my kids to memorize one day. But by the time I was done, I had narrowed it down to . . . the entire book. They need every verse in that book. I don't know how far we'll get, but they're going to know a lot of Proverbs by the time they leave the nest. Probably more than they want to. It will be the voice that nags them when my voice isn't there. You're welcome, boys.

The book of Proverbs is a dad writing to his son. It is personal and moving. King Solomon pleads with his son to listen to wisdom and live. And, as beautiful as the book is, he isn't just waxing poetic. He gets extremely practical. He tells his son exactly how to

- not be an idiot (see Prov. 3:7)
- work hard (see Prov. 6:6)
- be truthful (see Prov. 12:17)
- stay away from loose women (see Prov. 5)
- make good friends (see Prov. 1:10)
- be a good friend (see Prov. 17:17)
- be humble (see Prov. 8:13)
- be generous (see Prov. 11:25)
- speak well (see Prov. 15:23)
- stop a fight (see Prov. 17:14)
- listen (see Prov. 19:20)
- be self-controlled (see Prov. 25:28)
- find a good wife (see Prov. 31)

Most importantly, Solomon teaches his son to fear God. "The fear of the LORD is the beginning of knowledge" (Prov. 1:7). All our equipping, all our sheltering, is empty if it's not rooted in the fear of the Lord. Our kids need to know who God is and what he has done for them.

This comes with lots of talking and training. Sheltering our kids in their little years is about more than just closing the door to the outside world. It's about talking through situations with them. When our kids are young, conversation take the place of life experiences. My son doesn't have to get beat up by bullies in order to learn what bullies are. Instead, we can talk about it. He doesn't have to get hit by a car to learn about road safety. We talk about it.

Here and Now

Every generation thinks that generations in the past were better. We long to raise our kids in the "good ol' days." But, of course, there were no "good ol' days"—not since the day that sin entered the garden. Every generation has had its own unique problems and its own unique spin on the same old sins. When we long for an easy, pain-free, sin-free life for our kids, we're not really thinking of this world at all. What we're really longing for is our heavenly home. But God has our kids in the world, with all its earthly pain and problems, for a reason.

Paul felt the tension between the benefits of being in his true heavenly home and the benefits of being on earth. After comparing the two, he said,

> I am hard pressed between the two. My desire is to depart and be with Christ, for that is far better. But to remain in the flesh is more necessary on your account. Convinced of this, I know that I will remain and continue with you all, for your progress and joy in the faith. (Phil. 1:23–25)

Paul knew that his time on earth wasn't just a holding place. It was necessary.

When we feel the suffocating anxiety of having to launch our kids into a world we can't control, we can take comfort in the fact that God has a plan for them in that world. Out of the entire timeline of world history, God picked this time and this place for our children to be born. It's not our job to prepare the world for our kids. It's our job to prepare them for the world— the world that God chose for them.

I can think up all kinds of scary situations that my kids could get into when they're grown and gone (and believe me, I have). But that's when I take a deep breath and remind myself that God has plans for my kids that I know nothing about. I can't prepare them for every scenario I can dream up. But I *can* prepare them to know truth from error. I can teach them the fear of the Lord. I can teach them how to make good decisions— whether they will take my advice or not. That's in God's hands.

I wish I could implant a little chip in my kids when they leave the nest that would make an alarm sound every time they were about to make a bad decision. (That doesn't sound controlling at all, does it?) But there's no such thing. Instead, there's the Holy Spirit. He is the alarm bell that can protect my kids from bad decisions—and also *through* the bad decisions they do make.

It's not the four walls of my home that protect my kids. It's not my arms. It's not even all my good advice and internet research. God is the one who protects my kids. And just as he has the final say over their well-being while they're in my care, he has the final say over it when they leave my home. One day they will be out of my arm's reach and out of my sight. But they will not be beyond God's reach. The best way I can prepare them for the world is to help them to know the God who will be with them when I am not.

Glenna Marshall, author of *The Promise Is His Presence*, says, "You don't have to know why God works the way He does or doesn't. *You just have to know Him.* . . . Setting your heart on His faithfulness will settle your anxiousness, gazing on His goodness will calm your fears, studying His presence will comfort your loneliness."[1]

More than I want my kids to be safe, happy, and healthy in this fallen world, I want them to know the presence of God. And as much as I want to prepare them for life in this world, nothing is more important than preparing my kids for eternity.

Next time you turn on the news and feel that twinge of anxiety over your precious babies, remember these comforting words written by pastor Maltbie Davenport Babcock in 1901:

This is my Father's world.
O let me ne'er forget
That though the wrong
Seems oft so strong,
God is the ruler yet.

What Other Moms Are Saying

For all the times I worry about my kids' safety, in the end, I know God is in control. Their health, safety, and very lives ultimately belong to him, not to me! (Janet)

I went to public school as a kid. I remember studying apologetics on my own so that I would have an answer for all my friends who asked me about my faith. That really shaped who I am today. My parents motivated me with their love for the gospel. I hope I will give my kids that same motivation. (Rachel)

Systematic theology and worldview training in my childhood were so incredibly useful to me when I later went to a secular university. My parents weren't there to hold my hand, but their teaching equipped me with discernment when I went to my classes. (Jessie)

I think natural consequences helped to prepare me for the world. If I forgot my homework or waited until the last minute to do a school project, my parents didn't bail me out. I got the grade I got, and that was that. (Christy)

We have to teach our kids how to be adults while they're still at home and *before* they become adults. Starting around age eleven, I let my kids walk to the library three blocks away. When I'm in the grocery store, I let them go around the store and get things for me. My sixteen-year-old drives his siblings to school and gets his hair cut by himself. (Mary Lee)

My dad was a cop. He gave us real-life information to help us make good decisions, but he didn't try to make us fearful. (Christel)

Practically speaking, I'm preparing my kids for the world by teaching them safety. For example, knowing the difference between good strangers and bad strangers, never letting someone make you feel uncomfortable by touching you, and listening to your gut—if something feels wrong, it probably is. Get out and get help. (Janet)

I think a big thing to remember is that God is sovereign no matter where you are or where your kids are. We can't live in fear. It's paralyzing and isn't good for us or our kids. (Mary Lee)

Reflection

1. What is your greatest concern about releasing your kids into the world some day?

2. What is one practical way your parents equipped you for the world that you would like to pass on to your kids?

3. What's one practical way you can use your "greenhouse" to equip your kids to be on their own? (Focus on the spiritual aspect.)

4. Read John 16:33 below. What does this verse teach us about preparing our kids for the world? "I have said these things to you, that in me you may have peace. In the world you will have tribulation. But take heart; I have overcome the world."

5. Think about your kids' current situation—their home life, friends, school, and family relationships. Take a moment and pray for God to use what he's placed in their lives now, the good and the bad, to make them strong men and women in this world for his kingdom.

Conclusion

Created to Care

My favorite part of sci-fi movies is when the characters begin to realize they have been living in an alternate universe. Things start to unravel, and they don't know what's real anymore. It's fun to watch on the big screen, but it's not so fun to live in real life. That's how anxiety has always felt for me—like being stuck in an alternate universe. I see, hear, and experience everything through a strange filter. It's a filter I can't explain, don't want, and can't seem to change. It leaves me thinking, *There is something wrong with me. I'm not supposed to feel this way. This isn't supposed to be such a struggle for me. Is this my new normal?*

Perhaps you've had the same thoughts. You feel wired for worry and powerless to rewire your brain. I hope that as you've walked through these chapters with me you've seen that, rather than being wired for worry, you've been created to care. Your burden of anxiety is not pointless. It is directly connected to the tremendous, beautiful task of raising your children. And, as painful as anxiety is, we can use it to drive us to our Creator so that we seek his unending supplies of grace and help.

I mentioned earlier that nursing was a difficult journey for me. Some of my babies were easy to nurse, and some were nearly impossible. But each time I nursed my babies (or tried to), I was struck by the same thought: *"They have no idea how dependent they are!"* My babies didn't question where their food came from. They didn't worry about it. They just accepted it. My favorite part of feeding them was seeing their sleepy, content faces as they dropped off to sleep, full and satisfied.

Why do they trust like that? The answer is simple: God made them to. When King David was oppressed and desperate, he reminded himself that "you are he who took me from the womb; you made me trust you at my mother's breasts" (Ps. 22:9). Babies trust because they don't know any differently.

"But," I tell myself, "I *do* know differently. I know all the things that can go wrong. That gives me the right to worry. My babies don't have the responsibility and accountability that I do. That's why I need to arm myself with anxiety." And I feel pulled toward that alternate reality of anxiety.

But the point that King David was making is just the opposite. God sustained us before we knew that we needed sustaining, and we are no less under his care and protection now. My new set of "grown-up" responsibilities does not decrease my need for him or his care for me. I love the way Abbey Wedgeworth, creator of the *Gentle Leading* blog, describes this beautiful connection.

It seems like a poor design—that a human in its tiniest most vulnerable state is completely dependent upon a sleep deprived hormonal person with a foggy mind who is arguably at their lowest level of capability.

But it's a good design. Why? Because it takes a situation in which we may otherwise be drunk with power that we can grow or sustain life with our bodies, and makes us fully aware of our helplessness. I am as needy as the infant I nurse. I find myself more desperate for God's power, practical help, protection, and peace in these earliest weeks with a baby than in any other season. And that's a good thing.[1]

It's no accident that God entrusts us with such a big, precious responsibility while exposing our weakness at the same time. Our dependency reminds us of God's goodness. It reminds us that our care for our children is securely anchored in God's care for us. When I'm anxious about these precious little people who belong to *me*, I lose sight of who *I* belong to. I forget that I am God's "workmanship, created in Christ Jesus for good works, which God prepared beforehand, that we should walk in them" (Eph. 2:10).

We didn't create ourselves or our abilities. God created all of it. Our motherhood has God's stamp of ownership on it. This is his project. He is the star of the show. If you're like me, there are days you might feel like you're making it up as you go along—but every step we take was prepared by God. Our care for our children doesn't exist because they are needy. Our care exists because God is good. He created us to care for them. Our desire to protect them is from him. Our desire to see them happy is from him. Our desire for their salvation is from him. Every part of our care is part of the good works he prepared for us as mothers.

Every day I have an opportunity to remind myself, "This is a work prepared for me." This morning I discovered that the toddler had been shoving all his unwanted breakfast sausage into my purse. Unexpected and inconvenient, but a work that was prepared for me. At lunchtime my middle son needed discipline. Difficult and unpleasant, but a work that was prepared for me. In the evening my oldest son tested positive for strep and we came home late from the doctor's office with medicine. Concerning and exhausting, but a work that was prepared for me. Motherhood sometimes trips me up, but it is never unplanned. Every moment of my care for my children was laid out ahead of time. On purpose. By God.

Anxiety is not one of those "good works" prepared for us. Anxiety skews our ability to see those good works clearly. It tempts us to grab for a level of control that we were never meant to have. It gives empty promises of more peace and more security—all while pushing those very things further from us. God does not call us to be anxious. He calls us to care and to trust.

My favorite part of the day is the end. I love closing things down for the night. I love when every child is cozy in his bed, safe and warm. I lock up the doors, turn off the computers, and turn off the lights. Everything is quiet; everything is off. The only thing that doesn't have an off switch is my anxiety. There are nights when anxious thoughts that had been buried in the hustle and bustle of the day suddenly creep into the forefront of my mind. It would be so nice to flip a switch and turn the anxiety off, just like turning off the kids' CD of lullabies.

But God doesn't give us a switch. He gives us himself. His presence is with us when we feel safe and peaceful and in control, and his presence is with us in that strange alternate reality of anxiety. As much as we care for our children, *we* are cared for by a greater love than we can imagine.

So as you hold your children, don't forget who's holding you. When that familiar shadow of anxiety creeps in, pray, "God, you created me to care. Take the 'what-ifs.' Take this suffocating feeling of panic that isn't attached to reality. Take the insecurities that haunt me and the fears that blur my vision. You created this time for me and me for this time. You are with me, and your strength is enough."

Notes

Introduction: Wired for Worry

1. C. S. Lewis, *Letters to Malcolm: Chiefly on Prayer* (San Francisco: HarperOne, 2017), 35.

Chapter One: Peace for Mom Guilt

1. Doug Thompson, "Peter's Denial" (sermon, Middletown Bible Church, Middletown, CA, October 14, 2018).
2. John Bunyan, *Pilgrim's Progress: Simplified*, ed. Laurel Hicks and John DeKonty (Pensacola, FL: Beka Books, 1986), 71.
3. Martin Luther, *Luther: Letters of Spiritual Counsel*, trans. and ed. Theodore G. Tappert (Philadelphia: The Westminster Press, 1960; repr., Vancouver: Regent College Publishing, 2003), 86–87.

Chapter Two: Peace in Exhaustion

1. Kristin Tabb, "The Sovereign Hand of Sleeplessness," Desiring God, March 3, 2015, https://www.desiringgod.org/articles/the-sovereign-hand-of-sleeplessness.

Chapter Three: Peace in Prioritizing God, Marriage, and Kids

1. Jennifer Hicks, "Dear Mom on the iPhone: You're Doing Fine," *HuffPost*, last updated December 6, 2017, https://www.huffpost.com/entry/dear-mom-on-the-iphone-youre-doing-fine_n_5648388.
2. Kevin Halloran, "The 15 Best James Hudson Taylor Quotes,"

Leadership Resources, October 14, 2013, https://www.leadership resources.org/the-15-best-james-hudson-taylor-quotes/.

3. Ligonier Ministries has a helpful list of different Bible-reading plans. See Nathan W. Bingham, "Bible Reading Plans for 2019," Ligonier Ministries, December 26, 2018, https://www.ligonier.org /blog/bible-reading-plans/.

4. Michael Horton, *Ordinary: Sustainable Faith in a Radical, Restless World* (Grand Rapids: Zondervan, 2014), 193.

5. See Harriet Connor, "Give Your Children All of Your Attention. Some of the Time," The Gospel Coalition, July 19, 2018, https://www .thegospelcoalition.org/article/give-children-attention-time/.

6. I explain how anyone can create a sustainable routine in Sara Wallace, "Daily Structure: Why Routine Is Essential," chap. 8 in *For the Love of Discipline: When the Gospel Meets Tantrums and Time-Outs* (Phillipsburg, NJ: P&R Publishing, 2018).

7. Helen H. Lemmel, "Turn Your Eyes upon Jesus," 1922.

Chapter Four: Peace in Prioritizing Home, Church, and Self

1. Jen Wilkin, "Why Hospitality Beats Entertaining," The Gospel Coalition, April 9, 2016, https://www.thegospelcoalition.org/article /why-hospitality-beats-entertaining/.

2. Megan Hill, "Member: Connected to the Church," in *Identity Theft: Reclaiming the Truth of Who We Are in Christ*, ed. Melissa Kruger (Deerfield, IL: The Gospel Coalition 2018), 73.

3. Scott Slayton, "The Selfish Reasons We Skip Church," Church Leaders, August 27, 2018, https://churchleaders.com/outreach -missions/outreach-missions-articles/331883-the-selfish-reasons -we-skip-church-scott-slayton.html.

Chapter Five: Peace in Peer Pressure

1. Marissa Henley, *Loving Your Friend through Cancer: Moving Beyond "I'm Sorry" to Meaningful Support* (Phillipsburg, NJ: P&R Publishing, 2018), 29–30.

Chapter Six: Peace in Letting Go of Control

1. Elisabeth Elliot, *Keep a Quiet Heart* (Ann Arbor, MI: Vine Books, 1995), 18.
2. C. H. Spurgeon, *Beside Still Waters: Words of Comfort for the Soul*, ed. Roy H. Clarke (Nashville, TN: Thomas Nelson, 1999), quoted in Jared Mellinger, "Your Morning Will Come," Desiring God, July 15, 2018, https://www.desiringgod.org/articles/your-morning-will -come.

Chapter Seven: Peace in Discipline

1. For a full resource on gospel-centered discipline, including specific tips and practical tools, see Sara Wallace, *For the Love of Discipline: When the Gospel Meets Tantrums and Time-Outs* (Phillipsburg, NJ: P&R Publishing, 2018).
2. Chapter 3 of *Julie & Julia*, directed by Nora Ephron (2009; Culver City, CA: Sony Pictures Home Entertainment, 2009), DVD.

Chapter Eight: Peace in Our Kids' Physical Protection

1. Melissa B. Kruger, *In All Things: A Nine-Week Devotional Bible Study on Unshakeable Joy* (New York: Multnomah, 2018), 31.
2. Rachel Welcher, "A Surrender That Is Safe," *Joy Published* (blog), January 10, 2017, http://joypublished.com/a-surrender-that-is -safe/.
3. Beverly Linder, *A Never-Give-Up Heart: Raising Kids Who Face Harder-Than-Average Challenges* (n.p.: Special Heart, 2010), 14.
4. Linder, 15.
5. Linder, 126–27.

Chapter Nine: Peace over Our Kids' Salvation

1. C. S. Lewis, *A Grief Observed* (1961; repr., New York: HarperOne, 2001), 69.
2. See Lewis, 69.
3. Rachel Joy Welcher, "When the Unbeliever Departs," The Gospel

Coalition, March 7, 2016, https://www.thegospelcoalition.org/article/when-the-unbeliever-departs/.

Chapter Ten: Peace in Preparing Our Kids for the World

1. Glenna Marshall, "Not Why, But Who," *Glenna Marshall* (blog), October 29, 2018, https://www.glennamarshall.com/2018/10/29/not-why-who/.

Conclusion: Created to Care

1. Abbey Wedgeworth (Gentle Leading), "You know that phenomenon where you walk into a room and can't remember why you're there? Or you open the pantry and can't remember what you were going to get?," Facebook, August 22, 2018, https://www.facebook.com/gentleleading/posts/a.159156134567753/465118053971558/.